The CMIO
Survival Guide

A Handbook for Chief Medical Information Officers and Those Who Hire Them

Edited by
William F. Bria, MD, FCCP, FHIMSS
Richard L. Rydell, MBA, FACHE, LFHIMSS

HIMSS

The Healthcare Information and Management Systems Society is a cause-based, not-for-profit organization exclusively focused on providing global leadership for the optimal use of information technology (IT) and management systems for the betterment of healthcare. Visit www.himss.org for more information.

AMDIS

The Association of Medical Directors of Information Systems is the premier non-profit physician membership organization dedicated to advancing the field of applied medical informatics and improving the practice of medicine through direct physician use of information technology. AMDIS is the home of the "connected" CMIO. Visit www.amdis.org for more information.

Printed in the U.S.A. 5 4 3 2 1

Requests for permission to reproduce any part of this work should be sent to:

Permissions Editor
HIMSS
230 E. Ohio St., Suite 500
Chicago, IL 60611-3270
cmclean@himss.org

ISBN: 978-0-9800697-2-3

About the Editors

William F. Bria, MD, FCCP, FHIMSS, is a pulmonary/critical care physician and the Chief Medical Information Officer for the 22-hospital Shriners Hospitals for Children System. He is the President of the Association of Medical Directors of Information Systems (AMDIS) and the first Chairman of the AMDIS/HIMSS Physicians Community. He is an Adjunct Clinical Associate Professor of Medicine at the University of Michigan and University of South Florida. Dr. Bria has been a leader in applied medical informatics for over 25 years. He has authored numerous articles, chapters and books on informatics and most recently, he co-authored the book entitled *The Physician Computer Conundrum.* He continues clinical practice in pulmonary medicine at the Tampa VAH, Tampa, Florida.

Richard L. Rydell, MBA, FACHE, LFHIMSS, is a founder and CEO of the Association of Medical Directors of Information Systems (AMDIS), the premier physician membership organization dedicated to advancing the field of applied medical informatics. Mr. Rydell has a distinguished career as a healthcare executive, serving as a Senior Vice President and Chief Information Officer at Memorial Health Services, Long Beach; Stanford University Medical Center; and Baystate Health Services. He is a Fellow in the American College of Healthcare Executives and a Fellow and Life Member of the Healthcare Information and Management Systems Society. He served as National President of HIMSS and was a founding Board Member and Vice Chairman of the College of Healthcare Information Management Executives (CHIME). Mr. Rydell is the co-author of the popular books, *The Physician-Computer Connection* and *The Physician-Computer*

Conundrum. Mr. Rydell serves as an elected board member of the Seneca Healthcare District, Chester, California. He was recognized in 2011 as one of the 'HIMSS 50 in 50,' a recognition of 50 individuals who contributed significantly to the field of healthcare information technology and the improvement of healthcare through technology, in the 50 years since HIMSS was founded.

About the Contributors

Raymond D. Aller, MD, FACMI, FHIMSS, F(H)API, serves as Director of Informatics at the University of Southern California Department of Pathology, and as Clinical Professor at the Keck School of Medicine. A Harvard Medical School graduate, he has developed and implemented clinical systems during his Lab Medicine/Pathology residency at University of California, San Francisco, then in Santa Barbara and Long Beach, at the University of Utah, and in several regional hospital networks in the Southeast. He built the Automated Disease Surveillance Systems for Los Angeles County Public Health. Dr. Aller has contributed to several international standards (SNOMED, LOINC, HL7), has taught many informatics seminars at national meetings, and has published over 200 articles and chapters on informatics. His monthly national column on clinical informatics, "Newsbytes," is now entering its 25th year. He directs a range of clinical systems in the USC system incorporating four hospitals: LAC/ USC Medical Center, USC University and Norris Cancer Hospitals, and Los Angeles Children's Hospital, and has guided laboratory and informatics development at Grace Children's Hospital, Port-au-Prince, Haiti since 2008.

Michael Blum, MD, is the CMIO and Professor of Medicine at the University of California, San Francisco. Dr. Blum is responsible for the strategic design and implementation of clinical applications at the Medical Center. He is also an active clinician, specializing in preventative cardiology, congestive heart failure, and valvular heart disease. Prior to his medical career, Dr. Blum trained as an engineer and applies his expertise in technology to healthcare. He is currently overseeing a $160M enterprise deployment of an electronic health record and the development of a large-scale research data repository. He has a special research interest in clinical decision support technology and its impact on the quality and cost of patient care and population health. Dr. Blum earned his medical degree from New York University School of Medicine and completed his internship and residency in internal medicine and a fellowship in cardiovascular medicine at Yale. He is a fellow of the American College of Cardiology and a member of numerous professional organizations including AMDIS and HIMSS.

Marc Chasin, MD, MMM, CPE, is a family physician and Chief Medical Information Officer for the six-hospital St. Luke's Health System located in Idaho. Dr. Chasin has extensive experience as a senior healthcare executive serving as Chief Medical Officer and Executive Medical of Quality. He completed his Masters of Medical Management at Carnegie Mellon University in 2009. Dr. Chasin is a Certified Physician Executive and is a member of the Association of Medical Directors of Information Systems (AMDIS), American Medical Informatics Association (AMIA), as well as the Healthcare Information and Management Systems Society (HIMSS).

Steven J. Davidson, MD, MBA, FACEP, FACPE, serves as Chief Medical Informatics Officer at Maimonides Medical Center in Brooklyn, NY. A graduate of Temple University School of Medicine and the Wharton School of The University of Pennsylvania, he joined the newly recruited CIO and her team by participating in the 1996 implementation of hospital-wide CPOE and the 1997 implementation of hospital-wide PACS, and he led the 2002 implementation of a full Emergency Department (ED) EHR, the first in NYC. These and other efforts brought the hospital and MIS team the 1998 Computerworld-Smithsonian Award and the 2002 HIMSS Davies Award, and brought him the 2001 Physician Executive Award of Excellence from *Modern Physician* and the American College of Physician Executives. He has published extensively on quality improvement and physician leadership development in hospital-based disciplines. He sees patients with emergency medicine residents in the ED at Maimonides.

Richard Gibson, MD, PhD, MBA, is an urgent care physician and Chief Health Care Intelligence and Informatics Officer at Providence Health and Services – Oregon Region. He is Affiliate Assistant Professor in the Department of Medical Informatics and Clinical Epidemiology at Oregon Health and Science University. Previously he was Senior Vice President and Chief Information Officer at Legacy Health in Portland, Oregon. Prior to that he served 11 years as Chief Medical Information Officer at Providence Health System – Oregon Region. He received his PhD in Medical Informatics in 1995 from the University of Utah after completing his fellowship at Intermountain Health Care in Salt Lake City. He is a founding Board Member of the Association of Medical Directors of Information Systems (AMDIS). Dr. Gibson was previously a family physician and emergency physician and continues to practice urgent care medicine at Providence Health and Services.

Brian R. Jacobs, MD, is Vice President and Chief Medical Information Officer and Executive Director of the Center for Pediatric Informatics at Children's National Medical Center in Washington, DC. In this capacity, he directs the Children's IQ Network®, a pediatric health information exchange in the Washington, DC, metropolitan region. Dr. Jacobs is a Professor of Pediatrics at George Washington University. Prior to joining Children's National Medical Center, Dr. Jacobs was a Professor of Pediatrics at the University of Cincinnati, as well as the Director of Technology and Patient Safety at Cincinnati Children's Hospital Medical Center. While at Cincinnati Children's, he oversaw the implementation of their electronic medical record and was the principal application author and winner of the HIMSS Davies Award. Dr. Jacobs specializes in pediatric critical care medicine and has authored numerous journal articles, book chapters, abstracts, and scientific presentations. He frequently shares his knowledge in the pediatric space as a guest lecturer at conferences, leadership forums, and hospitals. He is a fellow of the American Academy of Pediatrics and the American College of Critical Care Medicine and the current chairman of the HIMSS – AMDIS Physician Community.

Howard Landa, MD, trained in urology at UCSD and Pediatric Urology at Texas Children's. In 1990 he joined the Loma Linda University to practice and developed his interest in medical informatics, becoming Director, Medical Informatics, in 1996. He joined Kaiser Hawaii in 2001 and became CMIO in 2005. He led the implementation of their EHR, attaining a Level 6 on the HIMSS Analytics EMRAM scale. In 2009 he became the CMIO of the Alameda County Medical Center, Oakland, CA. He has been the Program Director for AMDIS since 1997, was named one of the top 25 Clinical Informaticists in 2010, and is the President of the HIMSS Physician Community for 2011-2013.

Eric Liederman, MD, MPH, serves as Director of Medical Informatics for Kaiser Permanente's Northern California region, where he also practices internal medicine. He has served in leadership positions in applied medical informatics at several integrated delivery systems for 15 years. Dr. Liederman has published, and speaks internationally on topics including knowledge management, patient e-connectivity, collaboration with IT, and privacy and security. He received his Bachelor's degree from Dartmouth College, his MD from Tufts University, and his MPH from the University of Massachusetts, Amherst.

Jerome K. Wang, MD, FAAP, FACP, is the Medical Director for Clinical Integration and Effectiveness for the Cedars-Sinai Medical Network, focusing on the use of clinical decision support, process redesign and quality measurement systems for ongoing care transformation. After a decade of leading numerous EHR implementations, Dr. Wang is the physician lead for a clinically integrated community physician network within the Cedars-Sinai Health System, based on clinical quality, transparency and evidence-based practices. He is Associate Clinical Professor of Medicine and Pediatrics at the David Geffen School of Medicine, and has authored a number of peer-reviewed informatics articles on quality, clinical decision support and safety.

Contents

Preface

By William F. Bria, MD, FCCP

This is a pocket handbook for the new Chief Medical Information Officer. It will be a valued "quick guide" organized by topics that the CMIO deals with on a regular basis. The key to the value of this handbook is the accumulated experience and lessons learned of the AMDIS faculty that will contribute to its content. This book is also a concise guide to picking the right CMIO job and helping him or her to succeed!

It may never be known when the electronic medical record physician-champion graduated to adopting the title of 'Chief Medical Information Officer.' I lived through the years when discussions about first generation electronic medical records yielded quizzical or at worst, contemptuous looks from colleagues. However, now in the second decade of the 21st century, American medicine is poised to not only accept, but to embrace, understand, and leverage the healthcare information technology available to it and achieve nothing less than an information revolution in the practice of medicine.

At the time of this writing, a progressively greater number of young men and women are extending their training in medicine to preparation for leadership in medical informatics. It is to them that this book is dedicated, and to those who would seek to understand why they have made this career choice, to those who hire them in these roles, and hopefully to assist them in this transformation of healthcare.

The structure of this book is brief, targeted, and to the point, in keeping with the new literary style that has appeared in the last decades with the advent of the World Wide Web. It is our intention to periodically update and revise the contents of this manual, in keeping with the rapidly changing field of medical informatics, and the roles of the CMIO.

I would be remiss if I did not recognize the 30-year friendship and mentorship of Richard Rydell, the first Chief Information Officer to recognize the importance of this new role of CMIO. Additionally, the chapter authors, advisers, and wisdom that the Association of Medical Directors of Information Systems, AMDIS, provided for the core knowledge that we share with you today.

A CMIO's Perspective from 2011 and Beyond

By William F. Bria, MD, FCCP

When you tell someone that you are a CMIO, the most common response is, "What's that?" From learned colleagues to your mother, this is still the most common response to your proud declaration that you are a Chief Medical Information Officer. But this is about to change. As a result of more than 35 years of progress in the introduction of information technology (IT) into the practice of medicine and the last six years of national focus on applied medical informatics, you are about to experience a transformation in both awareness of your chosen path, as well as expectation that you can transform your healthcare system, hospital, medical staff, and colleagues from computer-curious to information-savvy medical practitioners.

The focus of this book is to help you achieve success in these ultimate goals, yet avoid the obstacles that a mainly informatics-agnostic American medical culture can put in your way. Even with 35-plus years of documented experience in applied medical informatics in the United States as a foundation, you will still need to blaze your own trail, build your own credibility base, and craft your own success, since, to paraphrase our political colleagues, all medical culture is local.

We'll describe some of the key tasks and characteristics that will define success as a CMIO and point out some of the "time-honored" pitfalls, so that you might avoid them. But let's be clear—there is no fool-proof path to success. Many varied medical cultures exist (academic, health system, community practice, etc.), and each will require a CMIO's deep understanding and appreciation of key lessons of local history, especially regarding adoption or rejection of change. As these are learned, the successful CMIO must then craft his/her plans for introduction, nay transformation, of any medical environment to applied informatics in a very specific and tailored manner.

Let's first talk about the essential characteristics of a successful CMIO: (1) Vision, (2) Leadership, (3) Planning, (4) Communication of Value, and (5) Perseverance.

VISION

That man's reach might exceed his grasp through the use of his machines (the latter paraphrasing Robert Browning) has always been the driving force for transformative change in any field; so it is with applied medical informatics (AMI). The good news, dear reader, is that you, much like the many who came before you, stand on the shoulders of giants. A foundation is in place based on two generations of AMI pioneers which you will be able to call on and with both a literature and a long history of experience look any colleague in the eye and meaningfully say, "My friend, we are not experimenting here; this is been done, and successfully, before."

Additionally, since the creation of the Office of the National Coordinator (ONC) in 2004, our nation has benefited from the vision of David J. Brailer, MD, Robert M. Kolodner, MD, David Blumenthal, MD, and Farzad Mostashari, MD, in crafting a national plan for AMI and in both defining a financial incentive plan and forging a strong link between AMI and the data-based practice of medicine. Nevertheless, it is up to you to foresee the special future that could transpire in your own medical setting, large or small, by the introduction of informatics. You will need to grasp and communicate the local potential for the improvement in medical care and inspire your colleagues and patients alike. Vision alone is never enough; however, without it, you will be lost in the detail and complexity of the task. Pyrrhic victories have been all too common in the American history of AMI.

LEADERSHIP

The American medical profession has, over the past 40 years, significantly changed in its diversity, authority, and societal position, especially regarding leadership. Being the son of a primary care physician practicing in the 1950s and 1960s, the romance of the medical practitioner, beloved by his community, tightly knit into the fabric of that community, and *defacto* leader in the community, inspired me to become a physician. In the 1970s and 1980s, primary care gave way to specialization, however, and emphasis shifted to procedural and increasingly complex (and expensive) healthcare, as providers and payers played a hectic race to outflank one another in pursuit of the financial rewards of medicine. The race was on as well for early adoption of the latest medical technologies. Evolution in the past 20 years now has the profession straining to maintain its past economic and societal position with financial pressures progressively undermining those old previous connections with community leadership and respect.

Leadership has always been a complex calculus and is specific to the domain/environment/population being led. Although General George S. Patton was the right man for the Battle of the Bulge, he probably wouldn't be the best leader of AMIs in a small community hospital (although we can dream). Even in medicine, the successful leadership qualities needed in a large academic medical center are significantly different than those needed in large rural group practice. Nevertheless, the assumption of the mantle of leadership in the successful introduction of applied medical informatics always entails effective planning, communication, and perseverance.

PLANNING

Planning the introduction of AMI unfortunately usually begins with the acquisition of an electronic health record system (EHR). Unfortunately, since the message that this usually sends to a healthcare administration and medical community is that "it's all about the computer" with the next step typically "find out what the doctors want and ask the vendors if their product does it." Finally, following purchase, the major agenda is compliance ("get the doctors to use it!"), creating an adversarial and inappropriate characterization of the entire AMI effort by the medical community from the start.

The human mind and spirit are flexible and optimistic, however, and these situations can and have been turned around in many communities and health systems. Planning for the significant change in clinician workflow and practice needs to be unapologetically communicated early and worked tirelessly before, during, and after AMI implementation. As a result of decades of fine-tuning of healthcare workflows to meet the temporal, financial, and logistical requirements of a previous American healthcare environment, the introduction of AMI into this environment now requires both meticulous planning and an agile intelligent change management team, sometimes requiring the very latest technologies to avoid a workflow breakdown that might otherwise result in the premature termination of an EHR program (the examples here are legion).

COMMUNICATION OF VALUE

The successful CMIO is not an EHR salesman but, rather, an interlocutor. Since you're now reading that word in Wikipedia, please note that we're referring to the political definition, which includes the quote: "An interlocutor is a formally recognized arbiter, or judge. Their position, as such, is formal and their opinion in most cases is binding." It is preeminently important that the CMIO be recognized as a physician first and foremost and, as such, a defender of patient safety and quality of care. Although the role often involves crafting a less traumatic pathway from paper to silicon for a medical community, it must always be understood (from both medical colleagues and administration) that the CMIO's compass is patient safety and demonstrable quality of care in all things related to the adoption of medical IT. The value equation is, with passage of the Health Information Technology for Economic and Clinical Health (HITECH)—of the American Recovery and Reinvestment Act of 2009 (ARRA) legislation—now more obviously having arrived in America, yet we have a long way to go in striking the balance between healthcare and economics and achieving the healthcare equivalent of *E pluribus unum.*

PERSEVERANCE

Although pursuit of the incentive dollars of "Meaningful Use"* (MU) has put all participants in AMI on a fast-track in acquisition and implementation and value demonstration in America, the rate of change of human beings and of complex inter-human processes and communications has, unfortunately, not been correspondingly altered. Although technology adoption by the average American has significantly increased in the last decade, for the foreseeable future, the timeframe for effective AMI adoption in all but the smallest and/or unusually flexible medical communities can be expected to be anywhere from 5 to 10 years. The word *effective* is the operative one here and refers to achieving demonstrable improvements in quality and safety of care that really define the value of AMI and define the success of those who lead these efforts (e.g., the CMIO). In the short-term, this means that all CMIOs must set expectations for both their superiors and subordinates that this is a long-term commitment to change and workflow redesign—and furthermore that the need for information (collection, analysis, reporting) is absolutely essential from the beginning of an AMI program. The establishment of a quality information process is the responsibility of the CMIO and directly connects him/her to the CMO, CIO, and other leadership colleagues.

---

* HITECH requires that physicians demonstrate "meaningful use" of EHR systems in order to receive related incentives.

CHAPTER 1

The Evolution of the CMIO in America

By Ray Aller, MD, FACMI, FHIMSS, F(H)API,
and Richard Rydell, MBA, FACHE, LFHIMSS

The CMIO position is one of the newest executive positions in American healthcare. The creation of this role can be understood as a maturing of the healthcare industry in the U.S., especially in the application of IT in the practice of medicine.

Although the term CMIO was not widely used until the late 1990s, and most institutions did not formally appoint anyone to such a post until early 2000, some physicians were performing this role in the 1970s and 1980s and even in the 1960s. This chapter focuses on those individuals, some of whom are identified, and others who are more generally described, as they wish to remain anonymous. We cite those examples with which we are most familiar; there are numerous others who could be discussed, but we lack the knowledge and space to do so here.

Those who have practiced the CMIO role have depended heavily on the historic development of clinical informatics as a discipline by such renown individuals as Lawrence L. Weed, MD, at the University of Vermont in Burlington, who conceived of the problem-oriented medical record, a way of looking at medical information that has provided the underpinnings for all of our work in electronic medical records (EMRs). Similarly, Octo Barnett, MD, and his team at Massachusetts General Hospital (MGH) in Boston had the brilliant insight to understand that medical data had unique characteristics and to conceive of the MUMPS (Massachusetts General Hospital Utility Multi-programming System) database structure, alternatively known as M, and related tools, which have served as the underpinnings for the most successful and widely deployed large-scale medical software programs, such as Veterans Administration's Decentralized Hospital Computer Program (DHCP), Veterans Health Information Systems and Technology Architecture (VistA), EPIC, Sunquest, Medical Information Technology (Meditech), and many others. Donald W. Simborg, MD, of the University of California at San Francisco, envisioned the need for peer-based communications protocols such as Health Level 7 (HL7). Roger A. Cote, MD, DSc (Hon), and the Systematized Nomenclature of Medicine- [Clinical terms was only added 35 years later, with "-CT"] (SNOMED) Committee built and championed our key tool for semantic interoperability. Clem McDonald, MD, led the development of real-world interoperability, through protocols (lab communications), semantics (the Logical Observation Identifiers Names and Codes [LOINC] database and universal standard), and reality (the Indiana Health Information Network). We could list dozens more. But these are the subject pioneers—the CMIOs who have created or taken these tools and made them real in their own institutions. The accounts of some of these innovators are included in this chapter.

The earliest creation of an organization-wide EMR system was a 1968–1972 experiment funded by the U.S. Department of Health, Education, and Welfare—a collaboration between Lockheed Corporation many of whose engineers and programmers had created the U.S. Gemini space program—and El Camino Hospital in Mountain View, CA. Particularly important to the implementation of this EMR tool at El Camino was Dr. Ralph Watson, who truly embodied the position of CMIO decades before anyone used the term.

In order to better understand how physicians, nurses, and others in healthcare were actually using the medical chart and communications tools, a young hospital administrator, Richard L. Rydell, MBA, set up super-eight movie film with a time code at a busy nursing station at El Camino Hospital. With time lapse recordings, this pioneer was able to discover what clinicians' communications entailed in the daily process of care and, importantly, how long they took in each of the activities. In retrospect, it is remarkable to realize that they were focused on the improvement of the process of workflow and provider communications, which remains to this day one of the most elusive aspects of EMR implementation.

Although the Lockheed (later Technicon) system implemented in El Camino was implemented in several other hospitals over the next two decades (including the Clinical Centers of the National Institutes of Health [NIH]), the time wasn't yet ripe for the widespread deployment of clinical information systems (CISs).

Another example of physician leadership of hospital informatics unfolded beginning in 1980, when a hospital-based physician arriving at a respected 400-bed community hospital immediately tackled the challenge of bringing the hospital from a punch-card-based Burroughs billing system (the only computer in the hospital) to an array of badly needed clinical and ancillary systems, this accomplishment a result of his unique combination of university, medical school, and residency training in clinical informatics. He organized site visits, encouraged system evaluations, and by 1985, the hospital was nationally recognized for the excellence of its laboratory, radiology, clinical, and pharmacy systems. Although Baxter Corporation pointed out to hospital administrators that the hospital now had the most complete clinical implementation of the Dynamic Control/Delta order entry/results reporting system in the U.S., the hospital repeatedly refused to reflect any compensation for his time in their regular (management-fee) payments to his medical group. Although his partners made it clear that they couldn't continue to permit him to work on tasks "that we are not being paid for," hospital administration repeatedly refused to designate a portion of that payment for clinical informatics, steadfastly insisting that they weren't required to pay for informatics services.

Subsequently, the physician moved his practice to another city. The hospital, lacking physician informatics guidance, went on to purchase a costly and disastrous failure of a system for physician outreach. A few years later, the hospital was a major participant in one of the most costly and spectacular regional health information organization (RHIO) failures on record.

Fortunately, other community hospitals took an opposite approach. In 1982, Bill Bria, MD, a pulmonary specialist who had trained at MGH, joined the pulmonary division at Baystate Medical Center in Springfield, MA. Finding that the mainframe computer used there was useless—five years after implementation, its only clinical function was to order chest x-rays—Bria introduced the subject of its inefficiency, with indignation, at a medical staff meeting, putting into motion the dynamic that when one brings up issues, he or she is then charged with finding the solution.

News of his criticism reached the new Chief Information Officer (CIO) at Baystate, Richard Rydell, referred to earlier, who also learned of Bria's (successful) Apple II programming course for physicians. At their first meeting, Rydell's opener to Bria was "Would you like to do something about the problem you've identified, or do you want to just continue to complain?" After consultation with the Chief of Staff (Martin Broder, MD) and Chief of Pulmonary (John Landis, MD), Bria accepted Rydell's challenge to dedicate 25 percent of his work time and salary in order to take on the challenge as a physician champion in the information services department. Within a year, this dedicated time increased to 50 percent, and under Rydell's direction, Bria traveled throughout the United States, speaking about and beginning to understand what this task was really about.

Needless to say, Baystate has had far greater and sustained success than the shortsighted hospital discussed in the previous example.

In 1990, the Chief Executive Officer (CEO) of Long Beach Memorial Medical Center (Long Beach, CA) had decided to bring in the Technicon system (described earlier) because of its emphasis on the value of direct physician order entry (a dozen years before this became fashionable). He brought a Chief Information Officer (CIO) with experience in that deployment (again, the innovator, Richard Rydell), who in turn identified a highly respected member of the medical staff, Harris Stutman, MD, to serve as CMIO (although the term wasn't in use at that time). Additional physicians were recruited, all on a part-time basis, and within a few years the hospital had launched TDS7000, with a rate of computerized physician order entry (CPOE) as high as 80 percent in some specialties.

There are a number of examples of academics heavily involved in medical informatics in the 1970s and 1980s. In a few cases, they functioned as CMIOs, guiding hospital efforts in systems deployment, and in other instances, they focused on research and had little or no contact with the clinical side.

Most notable are those who stepped forward and developed clinical systems that became the core applications in their academic medical centers. One of the first, and continuing to be an important contributor to the clinical mission of the MGH, was Octo Barnett, MD, founder and still leader of the Laboratory for Computer Science. As mentioned earlier, his most far-reaching innovation was the invention in the late 1960s of the MUMPS programming language, which was used to create a clinical laboratory information system, a radiology system, a medication ordering system (decades before its time), a surgical pathology system (that served as a prototype for many of the systems popular today), a Computer Stored Ambulatory Record (precursor of today's EMRs), and many other clinically relevant tools.

At Indiana University's Regenstrief Institute, Clem McDonald, MD, and his team began creating the EMRs tool that became the core application for the Wishard Hospital and many other applications. An even more important part of Dr. McDonald's role was in his creation and championing of standards crucial for our interconnected world—the ASTM/HL7 (American Society for Testing and Materials and Health Level 7) standard for reporting observations, and the LOINC standard for naming lab results.

At the University of Utah LDS Hospital, Homer Warner, MD, PhD, and his team built a series of clinical tools, encapsulated in the HELP system, that became the beacon for such understanding (and application) as how to improve patient outcomes with informatics tools. In the early 1970s, they also constructed the Medlab laboratory information system, one of the first widely installed (and highly functional) laboratory information systems. Unfortunately, the adage that "a prophet is without honor only in his own country" applied to that team. For all the success they had at LDS Hospital (and subsequently at Intermountain Health Care), their opinions and guidance were often disregarded at the "official" University Hospital across town.

At another Harvard Hospital, Beth Israel, Warner Slack and Howard Bleich, both MDs, led their team to create a complete suite of clinical applications, initially deployed in the early 1980s and still in use today. These served as models for the clinical applications subsequently developed at Brigham and Women's Hospital, that now is the primary system for Partner's Healthcare.

In 1976, the University of California, San Francisco (UCSF) hired Donald W. Simborg, MD, as their CIO. Not only was it highly unusual to hire a physician for such a post, but this appointment occurred in what proved to be a highly propitious time. Dr. Simborg proceeded to develop a series of applications for important clinical functions (such as patient master index, surgical pathology, etc.) but also came to recognize the most fundamental needs for technical interoperability. It was out of this experience that he founded Simborg Systems and developed the first set of tools to freely interchange clinical data among disparate systems. Simborg's experience was one of the most important factors leading to the creation of the HL7 data interchange standard. In this instance, not only did Dr. Simborg's contributions benefit the patients at UCSF, but UCSF contributed to all of our ability to interchange clinical data.

So, several academic informatics programs became involved clinically, or built applications that became core to their medical center, while others, referred to earlier, remained preoccupied with academic research projects and largely oblivious to the mission of the medical center they inhabited. To differentiate these two tendencies, one need only consider how many applications developed by that group are being widely applied for patient care in their own institution, or in others.

In other academic institutions, physicians sometimes took the lead in acquiring and implementing commercial systems. One of the most notable was Mel Bernstein, MD's comprehensive installation of Meditech applications in 1980 at the University of British Columbia at Vancouver. Dr. Bernstein's vision of an integrated solution serving multiple departments off a single database was an inspiration to many.

Several physicians have assumed key roles in the development of the Veterans Administration's (VA) Decentralized Hospital Computer Program (DHCP), referred to earlier, which evolved to the VistA system. This has for several years been generally recognized as the most comprehensive and effective medical information system in the U.S.

The history of the evolution of the CMIO in the U.S. is largely a matter of oral tradition. And in recognizing this, we would be delighted if readers would contribute to us the stories of others who were early pioneers in demonstrating the value of physicians guiding the clinical information strategy of medical centers.

CHAPTER 2

Reporting Structure– Organizational Structure

By Michael Blum, MD

The "C" in your prospective title (CMIO) seems to connote the authority and responsibility required for you to be successful in the job that you are considering. In theory, it places you in the "C-suite" and provides sufficient control or influence over strategy, budget, and policy. In reality, however, the title is simply a few letters after your name and the header on the job description. The organizational structure and culture are more important than the title itself. Hopefully, this chapter will stimulate you to thoughtfully consider the structure and culture of the prospective organization and integrate those factors with your personal characteristics and goals, providing a more meaningful evaluation of the position than when considering the title alone.

Speaking of titles, the question of the CMIO title versus the title of Medical Director, IT (or equivalent) is worth discussing. While distinguishing between a CMIO and Medical Director may seem like splitting hairs, it may be meaningful in some organizations. Appreciating that the success of a candidate is far more attributable to his or her individual skill and effort, depending upon local culture and organizational nomenclature, the distinction between the two titles can be very significant.

For example, at an organization with very few CxOs and strong clinical influence and respect, a Medical Director may have all of the access and influence necessary to be a successful senior executive. However, as discussed later in this chapter, at an organization with an extensive executive suite, or one in which clinicians are not well-integrated into the leadership team, a CMIO title can be far more important. The bottom line is that in order to be successful, you need fairly open access to the C-suite in which strategy, budget, and policy are determined. If you are not "in the room," your chances for success diminish rapidly. Additionally, in some organizations, there are significant differences in benefits (beyond salary) between "Director-level" and "C-level" positions. Bonus structures, retirement programs, and other health and welfare programs can all vary, sometimes substantially.

For the purposes of this discussion, we will refer to the position as CMIO but remind you to keep these issues in mind if the prospective position is titled Medical Director, IT.

In attempting to evaluate how you as the new CMIO would fit in, it is crucially important to examine the existing organizational structure and culture. Certain questions are obvious: Is the organization clinician- and patient-centric? Is there an obvious feeling of collaboration between administration and the clinicians? Or is it an "us-and-them" environment in which the CMIO is expected to be a clinical "voice of reason" to buffer the administration? Also, is the organization content with its standing and public perception? Does it believe that it provides top-notch healthcare in a safe environment? Or, is it a dynamic, changing organization that is continually remaking itself in order to achieve its goals? Understanding and evaluating these issues and characteristics will be key to choosing an appropriate organization and evaluating (or creating) the reporting structure that will support a successful CMIO position.

While a CMIO may be able to function in many different organizational cultures and reporting structures, there is interplay between the CMIO's characteristics and that of the organization. As a result, an organization and structure that might be ideal for one

CMIO might be miserable for another. In evaluating whether or not an organization and its reporting structure are appropriate for you, five basic questions need to be answered:

1. Is the CMIO role new?
2. If the CMIO role already exists, what happened to the prior occupant?
3. To whom do the CMIO and CIO report?
4. What is the relationship between the CMO and the medical staff?
5. How dynamic is the organization? How does it handle change?

THE NEW CMIO ROLE

As the importance of clinicians with informatics expertise was first appreciated in the late 1980s and early 1990s, positions were typically created within the organization's IT department, closely aligned with clinical systems project management. The candidates for these positions were frequently internal, either recent trainees with strong computer skills and interest or veteran clinicians with significant organizational gravitas. The percentage effort for these positions covered the spectrum from minimal commitment to full-time, highly engaged efforts. Many of these individuals were highly successful, leading systems implementations that improved clinical care, quality, and efficiency. They relied on their clinical experience, organizational knowledge, and the experiences of their peers at other organizations to avoid many of the pitfalls that commonly befall clinical IT projects.

These positions were usually mid-level management in nature, focusing on selection, planning, and implementation of a single or few systems (albeit often large and impactful). With titles such as "Physician IT Liaison" or "Clinician Informatics Lead," these positions most frequently reported to the Clinical Information Systems Director (or equivalent) or the CIO. Whether the organizations grew to appreciate the value of these roles and wanted to leverage the talents, or whether the clinicians outgrew these mid-level positions is arguable. At larger organizations in which successful clinician informaticists had established successful track records and significant responsibility and impact, positions such as Medical Director, IT (or

IS) and CMIO started to appear. Today, these CMIO and Medical Director positions are de rigueur at organizations that appreciate the importance of clinical IT in the quality, safety, and cost of the care they deliver.

Now that the organization has taken the leap and created a CMIO role, or can be convinced to do so, it is crucially important that you understand their expectations. To do so, start by understanding how they came to the decision to create the role in the first place. Were they led by a management consultant? Is it included in their organizational or IT strategic plan? Or, were they emulating another organization? Has a member of the executive team worked with a CMIO previously? As opposed to an organization that is recruiting a replacement CMIO, the less experienced organization may not have well thought-out ideas about what a CMIO can and cannot accomplish. Expectation setting in this situation is critically important, and failure to do so can lead to mutual disappointment. On the other hand, understanding the organization's expectations gives you the ability to exceed them and be successful.

THE PRIOR TENANT

It probably goes without saying, but if the CMIO position is not new to the organization, it would be very worthwhile to understand the circumstances surrounding the previous CMIO's departure. While there are certainly a multitude of benign explanations for people to leave jobs, considering that the nature of these positions creates a good deal of opportunity for friction between senior management and the CMIO, finding out the exact previous circumstances of departure may be advisable. While the data are not robust, the general sense is that successful CMIOs are staying in their positions longer than other IT leaders. In the late 1990s and early 2000s, the life expectancy of a CIO at an organization was only slightly greater than three years. In recent Gartner/AMDIS surveys, the tenure of CMIOs who are satisfied with their positions appears to be much longer, and they don't appear to be looking for the next position. So, while there may be a perfectly benign explanation for a vacated CMIO position, it certainly bears investigating.

Probably the best source of information in your investigation is the prior CMIO. While a mature executive will not necessarily lay out the issues for you, anything short of glowing praise for the organization and a believable explanation for his or her departure should raise warning flags. If an apparent lack of candor raises suspicions, ask whether there is a termination agreement that governs what he or she can say about the experience. Also, ask him or her for the names of clinical, IT, and non-IT administrators with whom you should speak to best understand the organization. It goes without saying that you need to talk to the Chief Medical Officer (CMO)/Chief of Staff, inpatient; perioperative; and ambulatory medical leadership, and Chairs or Chiefs of the major services and your clinical specialty. Ask them what they thought of the prior CMIO and what needs to be/can be done better this time around.

THE ORGANIZATIONAL STRUCTURE

As noted earlier, the CMIO role grew out of ad hoc clinician IT positions and evolved as the healthcare IT landscape became more complex, expensive, and littered with high profile failures. In the late 1990s, it became apparent that CIOs alone could not lead the planning, selection, implementation, and operation of large, complex clinical systems. The CMIO was viewed by executives as a logical "partner." However, the lines between the CIO and the CMIO were never clearly drawn. While the early IT clinician's success was typically measured by the CIO on vague metrics, such as the amount of complaining done by the medical staff, they typically brought additional talent to the table. Some of these abilities were more appreciated than others. Whereas the CIOs often appreciated the personal relationships that the CMIO had with the clinical leadership and their ability to triage clinical IT issues, their strategic thinking, planning, and change management skills were sometimes threatening to the CIO. Some CIOs had turf issues, and others were afraid of being made to look bad by the young, eager, networking, intelligent upstarts. CIOs who had earned their stripes on mainframes, minicomputers, and complex billing systems were put off by the clinicians who were less concerned with billing and cost accounting systems and were instead focused on end users, clinical applications, workstations, CPOE, clinical decision support, workflow, mobility computing, and unified communications—things often outside of the CIO's comfort zone.

Over time, with or without the support of the CIOs, the early IT clinicians grew into leadership roles in their organizations. As they became CMIOs and took on more strategic responsibilities and pushed for higher levels of IT service to the clinical community, they became less aligned with the CIO and more aligned with the CMO. Additionally, pressure from the CMO to leverage the new CIS tools to improve clinical care commonly created challenges for the CIOs, as the legacy systems' capabilities were frequently less than expected. The CIO's agility, interest, and ability to leverage new technologies were very limited. Many relationships between CIOs and CMIOs deteriorated, and the traditional reporting structure was questioned. As some CMIOs changed their reporting relationships to report to the CMO, other CMIOs, recruiters, and organizations asked whether the CMIO should ever report to the CIO. Doesn't reporting to the CMO make more sense? Should the CMIO have dual (matrix) reporting to both the CIO and CMO? If so, which is the solid and which is the dotted line? Also, in an academic environment, the issue was more complicated by the academic reporting structure. CMIOs need a home in their clinical specialty, which would give them three bosses— more than anyone should have to carry!

When considering to whom the position reports, it is important to consider your potential bosses' reporting as well. While the CMO most commonly reports to the Chief Executive Officer (CEO), it is not uncommon for the CIO to report to the CEO, Chief Operating Office (COO), or Chief Financial Officer (CFO) as shown in Figure 2-1.

The "flat" organizational structure shown in scenario A of Figure 2-1 provides the most flexibility in CMIO reporting. Assuming reasonably comparable political strengths and personalities of the other CxOs, and no significant bias by the CEO, a single report to either the CIO or CMO, or a dotted line to one of them can work in this scenario. Who gets the dotted and solid lines is a difficult question. Several factors must be considered, including the clinical orientation of the IT department, the status of clinical systems deployment, the sophistication of the clinical systems, and the expectations and technological insight of the CMO. In less mature IT shops with little appreciation for clinical needs and expectations, it makes sense to focus energy there, helping to develop the necessary clinical service model to support advanced clinical systems in the organization. On the other hand, if the IT department is fairly solid, clinical systems delivery is acceptable, and tools such as clinical decision support and business intelligence are on the roadmap or in place, your focus may be better placed in the CMO's organization to focus on system optimization and best support the CMO's agenda.

Figure 2-1. Organizational charts showing possible reporting structures.

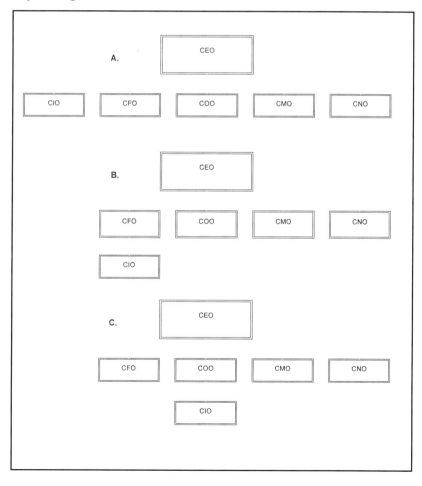

If the CIO does not report directly to the CEO (as shown in scenarios B and C of Figure 2-1), and your position will report to the CIO, there is more risk. In this scenario, you are another step removed from the decision making, and, in a strongly hierarchical organization, this positioning can be very difficult. Despite the CMIO title, you may not truly be in the C-suite nor at the table for important strategic and tactical planning and decision making. Additionally, in the current environment, a good deal of caution is appropriate in considering an organization that does not appreciate the importance of IT highly enough to have the CIO report to the CEO.

The most challenging scenario is the one in which the CIO reports to the CFO (scenario B). In this case, the CIO may have difficulty making clinical systems a top priority. Also, the financial shops can be change averse and may not embrace the move toward new paradigms that you will need to introduce. Organization structures with the CIO reporting to the COO (scenario C) seem to be the least common. On the surface, it seems to make more sense, as the COO should be more sensitive to clinical quality and efficiency, but the personal interplay between the COO and CIO will be crucial. Also, access to capital and operating resources may be more challenging, as the COO will need to compete IT's needs against those of his or her other reports. While that naturally happens to an extent around the capital budget table, if the CIO is subordinate to the COO, it makes it difficult for him or her to argue strongly in a semi-public forum without creating interpersonal issues and questioning of loyalty and teamwork.

In scenarios B or C, insisting on some level of reporting to the CMO is strongly recommended. In fact, except in rare circumstances (e.g., prior personal relationships or extensive organizational experience), I would avoid a position with one of these organizational structures without reporting ties to the CMO. A solid line to the CMO and dotted line to the CIO in one of these models would be preferred.

What about reporting solely to the CMO? Certainly, the concept is attractive as you have clinical experience and focus in common. The downside is the potential loss of influence in the IT shop. The CMIO needs to be seen as a central figure within IT by the department. He or she needs to be seen as a senior leader and decision maker who helps create a unified clinical IT vision and plan. If the CMIO is viewed as an outsider or another clinician who throws problems over the wall and points out poor performance, he or she will be quickly frustrated by the inability to improve the department. This issue would not be as significant in a setting in which the IT department is clinically mature and has a strong clinical focus. For example, in an organization that has had CPOE implemented with a high level of clinician utilization and satisfaction, reporting only to the CMO is reasonable, as your focus will likely be on more advanced clinical issues such as real-time clinical decision support and deploying clinical/business intelligence tools to the organization.

Another recently evolving wrinkle has the CIO reporting to the CMIO or a Director of IT (or Chief Technology Officer, CTO) reporting to the CMIO. The Director or CTO manages all of the technical aspects, infrastructure, and non-clinical applications, while the CMIO is responsible for the clinical side of the shop (usually through a Director of Clinical Applications). Currently, these positions are fairly unusual, with most CMIOs reporting to either the CIO or CMO. Also, while these newer structures are intriguing, they do not provide a clearer reporting path for the CMIO. With the CIO/CTO reporting to the CMIO, to whom does he or she report? The CMO is very unlikely to want all of that reporting responsibility in his span of control; the CFO is unlikely to provide a good reporting fit for the CMIO; and the COO is typically consumed with running an incredibly complex organization without having IT with which to deal. That leaves the CEO. While initially attractive, and in some cases workable, successfully reporting to the CEO would require an uncommonly hands-on Chief Executive. Otherwise, the CMIO would risk becoming completely administrative, removing the CMIO from the interactions and activities that attracted him or her to the position in the first place.

The wild card that you must consider in all of this is the executives' individual personalities. A self-confident CIO who values your input and realizes that outstanding subordinates only improve his or her lot will make a far better boss than a CMO who is disinterested in IT, doesn't appreciate the complexities and challenges of clinical IT, or is unwilling to spend the necessary political capital to accomplish change in the clinical environment. The reality is that each situation will combine some elements of each of these scenarios. The bottom line is that your greatest chance of success is when you are supported by a boss who is viewed as successful by the organization and who views you as a part of that success.

WHAT DO YOU WANT TO BE WHEN YOU GROW UP?

Your sense of alignment with the various players in the C-suite will be to some extent influenced by your self-perception and future goals. Ideally, the organizational structure should reflect those characteristics and ambitions. If you have a business or operations focus, enjoy having a significant span of control, and see yourself as a CEO or COO down the road, then an organizational structure in which you report to the CIO/COO/CFO would be appropriate. Conversely, a more "clinical champion" CMIO may struggle reporting to anyone other than the CMO. Obviously, if your goal is to grow into a CIO role, reporting there makes good sense. Whatever the options, carefully consider the tools that you have and the experiences that you will gain in the particular position and structure. Are they consistent with your near- and long-term goals?

In considering a position in which you would report to the CMO, an important consideration is the relationship between the CMO and the medical staff. These relationships cover the spectrum from revered leader to administrative lackey, from energetic advocate for quality, safety, and change to the guardian of the status quo. Moreover, the type of organization will determine the CMO's span of control and sphere of influence. At a community hospital with local competition and voluntary faculty, it can be challenging for even a strong CMO to make significant change. In an academic medical center with a closed faculty medical staff and residents on the hospital's payroll, the conflicts created by the research and teaching missions impact the relationship.

Regardless of the model, a significant amount of your ability to drive change will be related to your relationship with the CMO and his or her relationship with the medical staff. Ideally, the CMO sets the agenda for clinical change, creating a vision for an organization with higher quality, safer, more efficient medical care. Your job is to create the IT landscape that supports that vision. However, if the

CMO is unable to motivate the medical staff to accept the challenge of incorporating CPOE, electronic clinical documentation, or clinical decision support into their practice, then all of that work falls upon your shoulders. Being successful as a CMIO with a weak or technologically uninterested CMO in the setting of a contentious medical staff is not impossible, but you must recognize that progress will be far slower. If you are not going to be the inaugural occupant of the office, then when chatting with the prior CMIO, you will have an excellent opportunity to get a sense of both the CMO and his or her relationship with the medical staff.

THE ONLY CONSTANT IS CHANGE

As CMIOs, we are driven to make change. We implement disruptive technologies and create tremendous stress (at least initially) in our organizations. Successful CMIOs work in dynamic organizations that embrace change and relentlessly seek a better way of delivering top-notch, safe, efficient care. Organizations that are highly regarded in local and national rankings, but rest on their laurels, will have difficulty accepting the change necessary to accomplish what needs to be done. This is not to say that you as the CMIO cannot be successful in such an organization, but you will probably need to move much more slowly and be more patient. Organizations that are content with the status quo, are driven by a regulatory compliance agenda, and resist change, should probably be avoided.

CONCLUSION

Recognizing that the success of a CMIO is more related to the individual than the organizational structure, appreciating the environment that you are considering is still important. A superior CMIO might overcome many of the obstacles that a suboptimal organizational structure or dysfunctional culture can throw at him or her. However, as your effectiveness, accomplishments, and daily frustrations are highly influenced by the organizational systems and structures within which you exist, some situations would be best avoided.

However, if you are thoughtful and vigilant in evaluating opportunities, finding or creating an organizational structure that matches your personal characteristics, skill set, and goals will provide a strong start in a new position.

CHAPTER 3

Organizational Readiness for the CMIO

By Eric M. Liederman, MD, MPH

The purpose of this chapter is to answer the question: When is a healthcare organization ready for a CMIO, and what are the conditions that constitute fertile ground for a CMIO to be successful?

Healthcare organizations in the U.S. are in a variety of states of deployment of healthcare information systems, ranging from precontemplation (all paper and happy with it) to "paperless," with many states in between—including active, partial, and failed implementations, deinstallations, and changes of vendors. Where an organization is, where it has been, where it wants to go, who is making decisions, and prior experience with the position all play into the likelihood of success of a CMIO.

While CMIO job descriptions, titles, and reporting relationships vary, as described in other chapters, the ability of CMIOs to successfully deliver on organizational expectations is driven, in a large part, by organizational characteristics. Prospective CMIOs and healthcare organizations looking to hire them should attend to these issues, since the stakes involved are high.

Implementation, replacement, or expansion of EHRs and their constituent and contributory clinical information systems are organization-changing events, which:

- Highlight all the variation, nonstandard practices, and workarounds in an organization;
- Change the way every single person does his or her job;
- Vacuum up much more capital and operating dollars than planned or imagined; and
- Make clinical care and operations dependent on the IT infrastructure, as never before.

End-to-end organization-changing events such as these come around rarely. Since the opportunity they present to reach the next level of quality, service, and cost structure mirror their significant risks, it is critically important that the right leadership team be assembled and that organizational challenges be clearly understood and addressed.

RELATIONSHIP BETWEEN THE ORGANIZATION AND THE CLINICIANS WHO PRACTICE THERE

Physicians and nurses can scuttle, or seriously derail, an EHR implementation and have done so. Examples of significant clinician resistance to EHRs and CPOE include volunteer medical staff going to the press and state authorities, medical residents threatening to unionize, and nurses and other unionized employees going on strike.

Large change initiatives stress even the best relationships and can ignite simmering discontent. Collegial and collaborative relations between clinicians and organizational leaders are, therefore, a prerequisite for CMIO success. If a CMIO is expected to repair problematic relations in addition to leading a clinical IT change initiative, he or she can be expected to fail in both endeavors. Ideally, respected and effective CMOs, Chief Nursing Officers (CNOs), and COOs have worked with the physicians and employees to create a shared vision and readiness for change.

Danger signs include:

- A medical staff at war with administration;
- Significant labor unrest and labor actions;
- Bad press emanating from "rogue" clinicians; and

- A recent history of strategic change initiatives killed by a core constituency.

Organizations with significant unresolved clinician discontent should consider delaying bringing on a CMIO or attempting substantial clinical IT projects, and potential CMIO candidates should consider avoiding such organizations, until clinician relations are repaired.

STRENGTH AND EFFECTIVENESS OF CORPORATE GOVERNANCE AND MANAGEMENT

A CMIO is not an island; he or she must work effectively with many others within an organization to be effective. Clear, mature and collaborative decision-making structures and accountabilities greatly improve the probability that CMIOs will be successful in leading substantial change management initiatives. Conversely, weak governance structures, unclear accountabilities, and weak or absent engagement by key stakeholders can doom even the most talented CMIO.

Some key questions:
- Who is empowered to make what kind of decisions? Do the answers change depending on who is asked?
- Do multiple decision "centers"— and therefore vetoes—exist for some issues? Do effective venues exist for these disparate decision makers to achieve consensus?
- When people and bodies charged with making tough calls make those calls, do their decisions stick? What happens when someone tries to reopen a final decision? How effectively are decisions communicated and implemented?
- How connected are senior leaders with the action on the ground? Are they surrounded by filters?
- How well do the senior operating leaders work together? How are differences in approach and intent mediated?
- Is implementation of an EHR seen as a strategic business imperative, led by operational leaders, or as an IT project, led by the CIO?

CMIO candidates should consider avoiding healthcare organizations where leadership and management are weak or conflicted, where leaders are isolated from their daily operations, and where substantial change initiatives are viewed as tactical rather than strategic. Similarly, senior leaders and Boards of Directors should consider getting their house in order if some or all of these conditions exist, before recruiting a CMIO.

ORGANIZATIONAL CULTURE AND ADAPTABILITY TO CHANGE

The saying (attributed to Andy Grove of Intel, among others) that "culture eats strategy for lunch" is generally true. A corporate culture is akin to the personality of an individual—slow to change, rooted in history, and deeply biased. Culture determines how people within an organization interact with one another, engage with the outside world, and cope with change. Clinical IT initiatives, which bring tremendous change to all parts of an organization and require engagement with key vendor partners, can flounder on the shoals of a negative corporate culture.

Positive cultural attributes include collaborativeness, open communication, mutual respect, and a shared vision, mission, and identity. Problematic cultural attributes can take many forms and may include:

- Passive-aggressiveness, manifested as hiding information, frequent use of "yes, but…" as an answer, and a history of not finishing projects;
- Hyper-competitiveness, manifested as hoarding of resources, infighting, and backstabbing;
- Fear-based, manifested as blaming, a reluctance to speak out, siloization, and a dearth of cross-functional teams; and
- Feudal, manifested by a weak central authority and strong senior managers who guard their turfs jealously.

No organizational culture is purely positive, just as no individual is devoid of personality flaws. Since the change initiatives that CMIOs lead tend to expose and concentrate cultural challenges, CMIOs and other leaders should try to understand as early as possible the culture of their organization in order to predict and proactively address likely flash points. Commonly, a few vocal, long-serving individuals serve as the "keepers of the culture." Effective CMIOs will want to reach out to these people to address their concerns, or, if necessary, work with other organizational leaders to neutralize them.

FINANCIAL SOUNDNESS AND FLEXIBILITY

The EHR vendor market is immature. System architecture is often incompletely stable, code tends to be buggy, commercial content is of variable utility, and skilled labor is in short supply. In this environment, costs are likely to escalate far beyond initial estimates. The ability and willingness of the organization to access and deploy additional funds often makes the difference between a complete or incomplete (or failed) deployment. Some key questions:
- What is the strength of the organization's financial reserves?
- What are its options for accessing capital? What is its bond rating?
- What other capital-intensive projects are planned or underway in the time horizon of the EHR project?
- What is the medium term outlook on operating expenses (especially labor) and revenues?

If the answers to these questions are not positive, CMIOs and the technology projects they are asked to lead are at risk of running into financial crisis at a critical juncture.

RECENT EFFORTS TO IMPLEMENT ELECTRONIC HEALTH RECORDS

Failed EHR implementations are highly traumatic corporate events. As with other traumas, they require time for healing. Memories have to fade before the organization is ready to try again. At academic medical centers, the trauma is borne disproportionately by the housestaff, so at least three years must usually pass to allow most residents to graduate. At community hospitals with stable medical staffs, five or more years may be needed. A CMIO who comes into an organization too soon after a failed EHR implementation should be prepared to start with small projects to create a record of wins and to prepare the ground for when the organization is ready to try again with a big project.

STATE OF THE IT INFRASTRUCTURE

Prior to the implementation of an EHR, the only parts of a healthcare organization dependent on IT infrastructure are ancillary departments, such as lab, radiology, and pharmacy. Clinicians experience downtimes as delays in receiving specific types of information. Frequent planned and unplanned downtimes are common.

With an EHR, downtimes can severely disrupt clinical care by preventing access to all patient information, placement and receipt of orders, documentation, and messaging. System availability and IT infrastructure resilience become critically important.

Several factors can predict whether an IT department can successfully manage the transition to support 24/7 "real time" healthcare:

- How is downtime measured and tracked?
- How are disruptions analyzed: case-by-case or by reviewing trends?
- How are root cause findings responded to?
- How effectively do different parts of IT work together and with the clinical and operating departments they are supporting?

MEDIUM- AND LONG-TERM CAPITAL EXPENDITURE "WISH LIST"

EHR projects consume as much (or more) capital as building new buildings, but result in no physical structures to point to when complete. As with buildings, cost overruns are the norm, though the magnitude of the overruns is often much greater with EHRs, since there are far more unknowns. No matter how enthusiastic the Board of Directors and management are about approving the initial capital expenditures, the happy mood will wane as costs and delays inevitably mount. As time passes, the frustrations of other capital-starved managers will mount. The more that healthcare IT projects and CMIOs are protected, the greater the probability of their ultimate success.

Certain corporate characteristics will delay and reduce the predictable fights for resources:

- A robust IT infrastructure with up-to-date software and hardware versioning;
- Effective modeling and planning for expected growth;
- Broad alignment of incentives across the organization, including the personal compensation of senior managers, around the success of the EHR project; and
- A shared understanding across the organization of the strategic importance of the EHR project to the future of the organization.

If this prior groundwork has not been done, the attention, energy, and time of the CMIO and the IT organization will be directed away from planning, deployment, and optimization of critical healthcare IT systems to shore up the infrastructure. The resulting loss of time and increased expense will predictably reduce the momentum and likelihood of success of the core work the CMIO is asked to do.

CLARITY OF INTENDED BENEFITS FROM THE EHR

The more specific the intended benefits from an EHR are elucidated during the acquisition period, the more focused and effective efforts to configure the system can be. If governance and senior leaders agree to a clear set of objectives, the CMIO can lead the efforts to build those desired goals into the system. In the event that desired outcomes are not clearly stipulated, the CMIO will find himself or herself in the difficult position of managing demands from disparate interest groups and being ill-equipped to defend the continuation of the project at critical junctures, a final concern when considering organizational readiness.

CHAPTER 4

What Is the CMIO's Relationship with the Medical Staff?

By Howard Landa, MD, Michael Blum, MD,
and Jerome Wang, MD, FAAP, FACP

In the corporate world, a very common question is "who do you report to?" In that world, the answer may be directly related to your level of responsibility, influence, and even compensation. In clinical medicine, we don't usually think of whom we report to or who reports to us outside of the Medical Student/Intern/Resident/Attending hierarchy, but in organizational administration, it can be an important attribute of your role. In the past, the chief or president of the medical staff was commonly an honorary position with little real authority. Power tended to rest with those physicians who were the most productive, far enough from residency to be well-seasoned and young enough to be energetic and idealistic. In the corporate world, this might be middle-management, but not in clinical work. In today's healthcare organization, however, heads of medical staff are key power figures, and, because of this, it becomes imperative that as CMIO, you keep your credentials as a physician (remain "one of us") as you take on more and more administrative responsibilities (and begin to become "one of them")!

In any organization at a single point in time, the person you report to, those who you relate to ("dotted lines"), and the specific people who report to you—the reporting hierarchy—are what is important, not specific roles. But again, unlike as happens in clinical medicine, those people frequently change within an administration, so the roles you relate to become manifest over the long run. How the CMIO positions himself or herself within the medical staff of an organization can have a powerful influence on success.

HOW MUCH DO YOU PRACTICE?

Part of the characterization of a CMIO includes training as a physician. And by definition, one becomes a physician by completing medical or osteopathic school. But having medical credentials is not the same as having the experience of practicing the art of medicine; and this is what truly separates the CMIO from other individuals in information technology. As will often happen, when a CMIO makes a statement that others are fearful about making, he or she will hear the admonition, often by a non-physician, that "you can only do that because you have an 'MD' (or 'DO') after your name," while simultaneously acknowledging the need to say it. But as clinicians we know how little those first four years prepare us for our positions and how important our postgraduate training and clinical experience in the real world become. Don't underestimate the lack of understanding of non-physicians on this issue, although more recently, high-level non-physician administrators increasingly understand the benefit gleaned from having practiced medicine, especially in an environment ambient to the CMIO position.

Physicians who have not had substantial clinical practice experience bring considerable limitations. There may be barriers to acceptance by other members of the medical staff of an executive who has come directly from training without having had to deal with the business and medical realities of operating a medical practice. Likewise, there can also be obstacles to acceptance if the practice experience has been substantially different from that of those in the environment he or she is entering. A physician well-schooled in running a private practice in an affluent area may find barriers to acceptance to operating a Medicaid health maintenance organization (HMO), or an HMO administrator's knowledge may not be as esteemed to a university setting.

Additionally, the assumption may be that a CMIO is a full-time physician, but what does that mean exactly? We are used to the notion of a full-time physician being full-time equivalent (FTE). But what is full-time to a physician? It may be working three 12-hour shifts a week in the emergency department or five 8-hour days in a clinic. It may consist of floating shifts in radiology or 30 hours of office time during the day combined with 40 hours in the operating room, mostly evening and weekends. It is not our purpose to define the activities of a full-time clinician, but this needs to be taken into account when a physician considers the role of CMIO.

And, a physician must consider what it means to balance the demands of a physician with the demands of a CMIO. A recent study reported that, when polled, individuals reported globally spending an average of more than 43 hours daily (out of a 24 hour day! [an explanation follows]) with activities "including time spent sleeping, working, commuting, as well as technology/media-based activities."* Where will the time come that is needed to fulfill both roles?

Obviously, the only way to get these kinds of numbers requires the assumption that multiple activities are taking place within the same period of time. Examples of such multitasking include simultaneous conference calls while driving in-person meetings interspersed with e-mailing; and working while eating breakfast, lunch, and dinner! We are a multifunctional, multitasking, and at times, multi-mistaking society. Therefore the real question is: "Do physicians multitask well?" Watch an otherwise composed surgeon's frustration level rise when trying to answer a page, via a nurse intermediary, during surgery. How the easygoing practitioner's demeanor changes in a busy office when patients start stacking up and he or she is continuously interrupted by patient phone calls, EMR pop-up alerts, and a phone call from a spouse with a car problem. So unadvisable is this scenario that patient safety literature actually suggests multitasking as a prime source of preventable medical errors.

Does this suggest that a CMIO should not practice medicine while in his or her administrative role? In fact, one of the key areas of controversy regarding CMIOs is whether they should continue their clinical practice. The argument is made that the responsibilities of

---

* Available online at: http://au.docs.yahoo.com/info/PR/PR.html?ID=97.

the position are such that maintaining a medical practice requires compromising one career or the other. This argument is most frequently put forth by the recruiters and in some cases by the employers of CMIOs.

The job of the medical executive recruiter (headhunter) is obviously made much more difficult if the physician executive intends to continue to practice medicine. The recruiter must help the employer find a way to hire the CMIO and provide an environment in which he or she can practice. This can include such considerations as office space and staff, malpractice insurance, billing services, and issues surrounding bringing a new physician into a competitive medical community. Oh, and by the way, he or she will only be practicing part-time, exacerbating another issue: call coverage! Employers likewise have problems dealing with episodic unavailability and how to handle the income generated by physicians who continue their clinical practice. The rules that govern physician employment can make an otherwise straightforward recruitment quite problematic.

What may be overlooked, however, are the advantages provided to the organization by a physician executive who still practices the art for which he or she trained. So the controversy breaks down into two issues: (1) Does a CMIO have to come into the position with substantial experience practicing medicine; and (2) should the CMIO continue/begin a clinical practice in his administrative role? There are several benefits that emanate from a CMIO's decision to continue practicing. In the minds of most physicians, what truly defines a physician as such is whether he or she practices. Once a physician enters administration (starts "administrating" and ceases to practice), he changes from a clinician and becomes a "suit" in other physicians' eyes. A physician who is not practicing does not experience many of the challenges he imposes on the other clinicians. He or she is not directly impacted by the operational inefficiency imposed by poorly implemented systems and may not adequately perceive the financial benefits of an efficient billing system. He or she is insulated from patient complaints arising from inconveniences foisted upon them by poorly designed billing and scheduling workflows or employee dissatisfaction from these self-same systems.

There is yet another aspect of this issue that is not frequently addressed: since you are this far along in the book, you have probably come to accept that a CMIO must be something of a risk-taker. In order to create trust on all sides (medical, administrative, and IT staff), he or she will often have to take chances and stand for unpopular causes. By continuing to practice, he or she forever keeps career options open, allowing even more of a bold, unfettered role. Part of the armor worn by the CMIO is this ability to move back into clinical practice, usually without even leaving the organization. This puts him or her in a unique position compared to others in the C-suite. Although we have never seen a formal comparison, we believe that (1) CMIOs who continue to practice have a longer tenure at their organization; and (2) practicing CMIOs have a longer average tenure than other members of the C-suite, most likely because of this career option.

Looking at several scenarios in which CMIOs do not practice will help to demonstrate some potential risks of not doing so.

SCENARIO 1

A CMIO is hired from within the ranks of physicians within an organization. In this situation the clinician is presumably a respected clinician (by virtue of the fact that he was offered the position) and thus has less to prove to the medical staff. Given this background, is he able to leave practice and still be effective in the new position? Initially, he should be able to take a sustained hiatus from practice as he establishes himself in the new position, resting on the laurels that helped him ascend to the job. This type of transition has the one of greatest potentials for success in the absence of continued practice, but over time even this CMIO's star has real potential to wane due to clinical absence. As medical staff turnover occurs, and especially as new projects that require substantial change management proceed, the respect and support of the clinical leaders of the institution may become problematic. Changes that the CMIO is seen to impose on the medical staff without direct affect on that physician become harder to champion.

SCENARIO 2

A CMIO who has substantial experience in administration in general and in informatics specifically is hired from outside the organization. In this situation, the clinician has a proven tract record within medical informatics and this information and history is easily verified. The question of prior clinical experience is less important as she has a history of success in the field of informatics, though the type of medical organization she comes from may weaken this presumed expertise. If she did not practice in that past role, then starting up a practice may have near insurmountable obstacles; the CMIO may initially be able to take a sustained hiatus from practice, but major attempts at change and the management of that change can negatively impact the respect and support of the clinical leaders of the institution who may have been her biggest supporters early on. Again, change that is imposed on the medical staff without directly affecting the CMIO is harder to champion.

SCENARIO 3

A CMIO who has substantial education in medical informatics but little experience is hired from outside the organization. He may or may not have clinical practice experience. In this situation, the clinician does not have a proven track record within medical informatics and if he has a proven clinical tract record, it is outside of the hiring institution. Here, the reputation of the newly minted CMIO, as well as that of the organization's administration, is at substantial risk. Information technology projects, as many innovative ventures, have significant risks and failure, at least in some form, is almost inevitable. The absence of proof of expertise coupled with the isolation created by a CMIO's decision not to practice can lead to an overall failure of both the physician executive and major portions of the executive management team. This can have a ripple effect that endangers other undertakings (even non-IT ones) within the organization. It takes years to build the confidence and trust of a normally skeptical medical staff, and these can be decimated quickly.

So let me assume that I have convinced you that CMIOs should continue to practice in their administrative positions. How do they accomplish this? Let's look at three distinct types of CMIO clinical practices (or as is frequently the case, the three scenarios may also represent the evolution of the CMIO's role within the organization).

The first is when the physician still practices at near a full-time clinical load; say 70 percent or more of his or her time is clinical. In this situation, the CMIO usually has a more advisory role to the CMO, CEO, or most commonly, the CIO. He or she may or may not be compensated for this work, and as the old adage says, "you get what you pay for." The situation is inherently not stable over the long run. If the goal is the implementation or optimization of clinical systems, a greater amount of effort will be required of the physician and his or her team, and they must be compensated appropriately.

One potential option is to split the CMIO role among multiple physicians. This does have potential advantages but requires substantial organization, and this is not always easy with physicians. In this situation, physicians can bring different talents and experiences to bear on issues that arise. If they can be kept in sync with each other on significant issues, it will be much easier to ensure attendance at the multitude of meetings that benefit from physician informatics involvement.

The second scenario is one in which the physician still practices a substantial amount of time, say 25–70 percent. The CMIO is now a paid member of the administration, but when the amount of clinical and administrative work is taken together, he or she is usually working far more than those who work exclusively in either clinical medicine or administration.

The third common situation is one of a "boutique" practice in that the CMIO will spend a half day a week practicing clinical medicine. It is optimal to practice in a venue directly related to his or her role as CMIO. This enables their clinical presence to be witnessed outside their administrative roles and requires them to "eat their own dog food" (use the EHR they are championing). Unfortunately, due to the complexity of medical practice, this practice is sometimes done in a venue unrelated to his CMIO role, for example, at a free clinic or other publicly funded venue. This is the least optional mechanism for the CMIO to practice but is (slightly) better than not at all.

THE CMIO AND THE MEDICAL STAFF

Arguably the most important interaction the CMIO has is with the front line medical staff. These clinicians are the ones who will be most impacted by the CMIO's experience, intelligence, and foresight. He or she is the lead for change management within the physician community and simultaneously hero and villain, day in and day out. The level of trust he or she creates as liaison between the physicians and both the administration and the IT staff will directly relate to the success of his or her change agent role. The previous discussion regarding the CMIO's actions and those in the next chapter provide more in-depth discussion and call out specific tools for building this relationship.

RELATIONSHIP OF THE CMIO TO OTHER PHYSICIAN EXECUTIVES

One would realize after reviewing a number of CMIO job descriptions that a CMIO is charged as key physician leader in the initial implementation of health information systems but is also a partner to other physician and non-physician executive leadership in attaining and maintaining the benefits of clinical IT. Credibility and strong personal relationships with medical staff leadership and members of the medical executive committee, the CMO, Chief Quality Officer (CQO), Chief of Staff, and a significant cohort of influential practicing physicians is vitally important to being successful in this role.

CHIEF OF STAFF: PHYSICIAN ENGAGEMENT AND ADOPTION

Especially during the initial planning for EHR implementation in a hospital, medical group, or integrated delivery system, one of the key predictors of success is the extent to which the interests of the physician community can be fundamentally aligned with the process and goals of the initiative. Depending on the characteristics of the healthcare organization, the responsibility of securing physician buy-in does not fall onto one person or even a few physician leaders, although the

CMIO may truly have the most specific interest in helping to assemble a strong core of physician influencers.

An important ally in this team is the Chief of the Medical Staff (COS). In almost every hospital, whether academic or community-based, the CMIO must develop a strong working relationship with this elected physician leader and his/her successors. A trusting and credible relationship between the COS and CMIO can be a natural one, especially if the COS is particularly interested and passionate about the potential of healthcare IT in achieving medical staff goals. A fortuitous situation is one in which the COS has had prior experience with a physician-level clinical IT implementation, either in a physician office or in another facility. In this case, the COS likely has an intuitive feel not only for the psychological climate surrounding the IT initiative but also an experiential sense of the "players" that need to be engaged with an early discussion and some of the political pitfalls to avoid. The COS is an important strategic partner to the CMIO, but regardless of the COS' level of experience with the complexities of clinical IT implementations, the CMIO should maintain open communication with the COS and leverage this relationship to improve communication with the entire medical staff. This promotes an evolutionary awareness of the changes that lie ahead, helps align medical staff policies and governance, promotes incentives to foster adoption of the system, and harnesses physician knowledge and experience in making designs about clinical content and workflow redesign efforts. As the implementation progresses and incrementally impacts more and more physicians, this relationship especially will be important in maintaining a high level of communication and in responding to vocal feedback from the physician community.

CHIEF QUALITY OFFICER: SUPPORTING QUALITY INITIATIVES

A frequently cited driver for adoption of CISs is to improve the healthcare organization's ability to both measure and drive quality improvement efforts, either mandated by external agencies or driven by internal priority goals. In most organizations there are one or more physician executives who hold primary responsibility to drive the quality agenda forward. Although the title may vary by organization (e.g., Chief Medical Officer, Medical Director of Quality Improvement, etc.), for the purpose of this discussion we will refer to the person or persons fulfilling this role as the Chief Quality Officer (CQO).

As the CQO is responsible for demonstrating organizational performance in the areas of quality and safety, this physician executive should be keenly engaged in adopting methods and tools, either manual or technology-based, that enable robust measurement of clinical process or outcome improvements but also hold the potential for optimizing physician decision making during the course of care.

It can be assumed that most CQOs will enthusiastically embrace the adoption of IT as a critical foundation for future performance improvement efforts. This enthusiasm must also be balanced against a sometimes unrealistic expectation by quality stakeholders of how quickly and effectively EHR technology can help affect this change. Therefore, it is important for the CMIO to help temper expectations while not minimizing the potential role that technology should play in assisting the CQO and other executive stakeholders. The CMIO must establish a strong mutual trust and open communication with the CQO, while always considering the CQO as a key "customer" whose perspectives must be addressed during the course of the planning, implementation, and post-adoption phases. As an important partner and ambassador of the CQO, the CMIO should help communicate the clinical quality perspectives thoroughly in parallel to day-to-day project decisions and assume responsibility for properly guiding EHR project decisions to support existing and future quality priorities.

What are some tangible steps that a CMIO can take to successfully support the CQO in this regard? Especially if new to the organization, the CMIO must develop a deep understanding of the key organizational quality and safety priorities and challenges from the perspective of the CQO.

The following questions may be used by the CMIO to begin to build this understanding:

- What is the current breadth of the organization's quality agenda (i.e., The Joint Commission, pay-for-performance, CMS core measures, etc.)?
- What are the areas of greatest challenge in terms of performance improvement or maintaining current

performance? Which are mainly issues of data availability and which are primarily challenges of impacting organizational behavior?

- What new quality measures will likely need to be addressed during the next several years during the EHR implementation?
- What are your expectations of how the health IT initiative will impact quality and within what timeframe?

Using these questions and others as a springboard, the CMIO must engage the CIO and CQO to help define a joint expectation of how the EHR can substantially impact the organization's quality agenda and within what timeframe. It is perhaps even more important to not oversell the EHR technology as a cure-all for the organizational challenges surrounding quality or safety but rather as a necessary (but not necessarily sufficient) tool in the arsenal for quality improvement.

As a representative of the practicing physician community, the CMIO must also be a key negotiator in helping to balance the objective of demonstrating improved quality against the looming challenge of being able to achieve and sustain a massive organizational change incited by technology. Prior to implementation, the amount of workflow disruption and the resultant vocal clinician "feedback" must be carefully managed by political and financial alignment, strong engagement, and effective training but still remains a significant "pain" of any EHR initiative. Management and project decision makers will grapple with the known workflow risks of a healthcare ecosystem that does not rapidly achieve "full" EHR implementation but rather remains in a hybrid paper-electronic world for a significant amount of time. At the same time, they must realize that a more rapid and widespread change is likely to increase the amount of disruption that could impact sustained system adoption.

In the realm of quality improvement, the CMIO is in an opportune position to spearhead a similar discussion around the timing and extent of EHR-enabled quality improvement with the CQO and other quality stakeholders. In our experience, leveraging an immature EHR implementation and clinical decision support that does not facilitate physician workflow and adoption (even for such a noble cause as patient quality) is a risky proposition. However, weighing these considerations and developing a strong governance process involving the CQO, CMIO, and physician leaders must begin early, as there is considerable organizational learning and discussion needed to vet these issues and determine a proper fit with the organization's culture and context.

As these discussions begin and the implementation moves forward, the CMIO has an important responsibility to apply his or her knowledge and experience against the organization's attributes, quality priorities, technical constraints, and knowledge of clinical workflow to help support the CQO and other executive and clinical stakeholders in crafting a quality EHR roadmap. In our experience, these topics must be broached early and CMIOs must maintain a high regard for the importance of being able to provide an effective tool to impact the quality agenda.

CHAPTER 5

Setting a Course for Success for the CMIO

By Richard Gibson, MD, PhD, MBA

Candidates for today's CMIO role possess a wide variety of career aspirations and an even wider array of clinical, managerial, and leadership experiences. Organizations have widely varying needs for the CMIO, depending on existing organizational structure and complexity, and the history and status of clinical IS implementation. CMIOs would do well to prepare for the range of choices and expectations facing them. After personal reflection on goals, setting a course for success involves frank discussions with the CMIO's future superior, be it a CIO, CMO, COO, or others, all represented here as "CxOs." This chapter will discuss some of the likely duties of a CMIO and other potential responsibilities based on the CMIO's and the organization's needs and desires. We will discuss choices and performance indicators in those functions and how to be successful in each.

IT'S REPRESENTATIVE TO THE MEDICAL STAFF

The CMIO is the medical staff's voice in the IT department. The CMIO explains the IT department's sometime arcane strategy, functions, systems, and services to people whose greatest exposure to IT might be their own personal computer (PC) or searches on the Internet. The CMIO is the IT ambassador to the physicians, and the CMIO manages the IT department's relationships with the staff physicians—no one else in the IT organization is better positioned to accomplish this. The liaison function alone justifies the expense of the CMIO and propels the organization to go to all the trouble to recruit and fill the CMIO position.

In addition to promoting IT initiatives with the physicians, the CMIO serves as an input funnel from physicians back to the IT department. By rounding with physicians in the hospitals and emergency departments and visiting their private offices, the CMIO understands firsthand which IT functions are delivering value and which are misunderstood, unsupported, or even interfering with the care process. As far as unmet needs, the CMIO can see for herself where there are opportunities for new services or applications or simply new configurations of existing information applications. She is also in an excellent position to collect suggestions from medical staff members about what IT can do for patient care.

Sometimes the input from physicians will be strongly unfavorable. The CMIO will need to absorb criticism about IT from the medical staff. Listening patiently and attentively to all forms of negative feedback without grimacing or reacting emotionally can be therapeutic by itself in improving the acceptance by physicians of the natural limitations of IT. Calling the situation as you see it and admitting the weaknesses of the various current systems with honesty and directness builds the CMIO's reputation as an IT proponent with integrity and humility. It is crucial that the CMIO not oversell the capabilities of the clinical systems, which are still immature. The ability of the medical staff to rely on the CMIO for an honest assessment of the pros and cons of an upcoming system will tend to put the CMIO on the side of practicing physicians in their mutual desire to use IT to improve patient care.

GETTING THINGS DONE FOR THE MEDICAL STAFF

The medical staff understands that the CMIO is a proponent of IT. They expect the CMIO to lead the charge for adoption of clinical ISs. They will grant the CMIO license to claim more benefits than the clinical system may be able to deliver, while mildly diminishing the drawbacks of such a system. As long as the CMIO does not get carried away with this optimism, he or she can succeed in the role of salesperson. The medical staff and the CMIO know that at some point, the latter will ask the former to take a leap of faith in adopting a new system. The CMIO can enhance the likelihood of the medical staff acceptance by getting things done for the medical staff before asking them for their help. In other words, if the CMIO is effective in delivering benefits to the medical staff on minor issues and day-to-day operations, the medical staff is more likely to support the CMIO when the new system implementation is at hand.

The smart CMIO will be looking for opportunities to "take orders" from physicians. When physicians complain about system response time, help desk support, training, remote home or office connections, and the like, the experienced CMIO will pull out a piece of paper, take notes and promise to get back to the physicians within a defined time period. The CMIO that takes phone calls throughout the week from physicians will build a reputation of client service that can be relied on to engender medical staff support of new systems in the future.

Sometimes the requests or complaints from physicians can be addressed simply by the CMIO making a few calls to IT department staff to request minor adjustments. At other times, however, physicians will request enhancements of existing systems or new electronic reports from the transaction systems. These tasks can sometimes take many hours of IT staff time and may require purchasing outside consulting help. If the CMIO has a discretionary capital and operating budget to cover such exigencies, then he or she can powerfully commit to solving physician problems as they are presented at the various medical staff meetings. Of course, the CMIO will need to keep the annual budget in mind and think about whether the one-time request by a certain physician is worthy of new expense when compared with all the requests to be taken over the coming year. It is just that sort of judgment that can make the CMIO position extremely valuable to the organization and to the clinicians and can build a reputation of the CMIO as a "can-do" administrator. Even without a discretionary budget, the CMIO can still be well-regarded by his or her peers. He or she will need to come back to the organization and present and advocate for the request from the staff physicians, and the proposal will necessarily need to compete with all the other ad hoc requests made of the firm. The CMIO will need to come back to the staff physicians and directly deliver the good or bad news of the resourcing decision.

THE VALUE OF A PHYSICIAN INFORMATION SERVICES TEAM

As noted earlier, the CMIO will be called upon to handle physician requests, some of which may involve substantial effort by members of the IT team. In addition to having a discretionary capital and/or operational budget, it is very helpful for the CMIO to have a Physician Information Services Team dedicated to meeting the needs of physicians. Many organizations are dealing with a voluntary (private) medical staff in addition to physicians employed by the organization. The CMIO has an opportunity to set the scope of functions and the service level for private physicians. Caution is advised lest the promises made to physicians become unsupportable. It is important for the IT department to deliver a consistent and reliable service level that can be maintained indefinitely without asking too much of the IT staff. The CMIO is in an excellent position to assess the value equation for the organization of providing potentially exhaustive services for occasionally demanding private physicians.

In setting up a Physician Information Services Team, the CMIO can manage the team himself or pair with an operational manager who does the routine managerial duties like hiring and annual performance reviews. However, if the CMIO aspires to greater leadership and management positions, personally building and managing the Physician Information Services Team is a great place to start. The CMIO as a small team manager will develop experience in assessing the capabilities of individual staff members and promoting productive interplay among the team's staff with greatly different backgrounds including clinical, administrative, and technical skills. A critical discussion between the CMIO and his or her manager is required to position the CMIO in the management hierarchy, to provide adequate budgeting for staff additions, and to understand the long-term career goals of the CMIO. Many physicians have had little experience in management prior to their CMIO job, and CxOs are understandably reluctant to give new CMIOs too long of a management rope.

THE CMIO AS A SENIOR MANAGER

Many CMIOs and CxOs are likely to be comfortable with the CMIO as manager of a small Physician Information Services Team. The CMIO-CxO relationship may be challenged, however, when the CMIO aspires to a greater management role. The CMIO may want to take on responsibility of an entire clinical applications team, a data reporting team supporting quality management, the help desk, a training team, a PC technician team, the remote access team, and the like. The CMIO will then be competing with career IT managers and directors, which may strain relationships. With increased management comes increased responsibility to take part in human resources affairs, budget planning and management, staff hiring and firing, staff training plans, annual reviews, employee surveys, employee complaints, and other management duties. CMIOs may feel that either they are not qualified to do this work or that this work is beneath them, or that their time is better spent managing the clinical-technology interface. Becoming a good manager takes a great deal of time, time that could also be spent meeting with physicians, reviewing clinical IS plans, upgrading order sets, and so forth. The CxO may be reluctant to make exceptions for the CMIO when the usual management responsibilities are required of other managers and directors. Most CxOs can find people with non-physician backgrounds and non-physician salary requirements to become managers, directors, and senior directors in IT. Yet only a physician with technical and people skills can handle the medical staff interface for the organization. Thus another important discussion needs to occur between the CMIO and his boss about the former's long-term career plans and the latter's needs.

PROJECT FUNDS VERSUS DISCRETIONARY FUNDS

The CMIO is likely to be involved in a number of IT projects over his or her career. As the CxO gains confidence in the CMIO, the latter may be expected to begin to manage larger and larger project-related funds, including capital, one-time operational, and ongoing operational resources. These funds may or may not include salaries and benefits for IT staff. Well-written project charters and periodic status reports should provide adequate feedback to the CxO of how the CMIO is doing at managing money. Project funds tend to have a fairly short period of obligation and relatively limited risk for the organization. However, if the CMIO aspires to greater management responsibilities beyond projects, the CMIO will need to gain responsibility for managing ongoing operational and capital budgets. Such budgeting may give the CMIO greater discretionary judgment about funding ad hoc project requests, but it does expose the organization to greater financial risk if the CMIO is inexperienced. The CMIO will likely need coaching either from his or her superior or from an experienced member of the IT or finance staff.

NEGOTIATING AUTHORITY FOR THE CMIO

Whether or not he or she assumes the duties of operational staff management, negotiation is a valuable skill for the CMIO. As noted earlier, the CMIO will likely be present at many meetings with medical staff, Quality Management, Research and Development, and others. Being able to effectively negotiate with other organizational leaders on IT responsibilities and clinical system adoption is a core duty of the CMIO. But it is crucial that the CMIO have his manager's backing and guidance, so that the CMIO does not commit the IT department to perform beyond its operational capabilities. It may take years for the CMIO to develop the confidence of medical staff and organizational leaders, but it can be lost in a few seconds if the CMIO overcommits and underdelivers. It would be easier, perhaps, for the CxO to be at that meeting himself and negotiate the commitment, but this is inefficient for the organization and fails to develop the skills of the CMIO.

Similarly, the CMIO may be in an excellent position to negotiate with an external vendor for clinical IS products. A seasoned CMIO will have an excellent sense for the value of a new clinical product, the challenge of adoption, the need for training the IT staff and end users, and the long-term operational expense of the system. Of course, the vendor needs to know that the CMIO is in a position of authority to negotiate for the organization, and this can only come about if the CxO and CMIO have had another candid discussion. Beyond just the intent and authority to negotiate, the CxO must be willing to coach or arrange for coaching of the CMIO in building negotiation skills.

OVERLAPPING DUTIES OF THE CXO AND CMIO

As the organization enters into more clinical IS purchases and implementations, ongoing management, and quality and outcome reporting, the CMIO and his manager will increasingly find that they are attending many of the same meetings. If the CxO and CMIO do not explicitly manage this overlap, the CxO is likely to feel that she is not getting full value from the CMIO, and the CMIO is likely to feel constrained and underdeveloped. The CMIO and his superior need frequent one-on-one meetings to evaluate the need for one or the other to appear at standing organizational meetings. Agreement must also be reached on limits of designing, planning, commitment, budgeting, and negotiation authority. This will require the CxO to be comfortable delegating to the CMIO along with the attendant responsibility to nurture and develop the CMIO's skills.

During clinical system implementation, the CMIO is likely to be significantly involved with the clinical applications team, the technical teams including server management, network management, desktop engineering, and PC support, as well as quality and patient safety monitoring, and business unit reporting often handled outside of the IT department. The CMIO will need clear direction from her manager whether the CMIO attends those meetings as an advisor or attends as a signing authority. Will anything suggested by the CMIO have to be approved by her boss after the meeting? Such responsibilities can develop the management and organizational skills of the CMIO, but it takes a highly communicative and emotionally intelligent CxO to allow the CMIO to flourish.

THE CHIEF NURSING INFORMATION OFFICER

As organizations become more involved with clinical ISs, they will need nurses in positions of responsibility opposite the CMIO. The CMIO and Chief Nursing Information Officer (CNIO) will obviously need to work closely together and coordinate their many areas of overlap. To whom should the CNIO report? Are physician and nurse leaders in the organization considered peers? How many direct reports can the CxO take on? Depending on organizational tenure, clinical IS responsibility, and management experience, it may be entirely appropriate for the CMIO to report to the CNIO, or the CNIO to report to the CMIO, or for them both to report to a CIO, COO, or CQO. In any case, the three executives will need to have a candid discussion about what is best for the patients, the organization, and the careers of the physician and nurse.

CLINICAL PRACTICE FOR THE CMIO

CMIOs may wish to retain their clinical duties while assuming the administrative tasks of the CMIO. A number of CMIOs will want to retain halftime status in their clinical field, but as their duties within ISs increase, it will become harder and harder for them to accomplish their IT goals with only 50 percent time available to the IT department. Depending on the CMIO's clinical specialty, she may or may not be able to continue to perform clinically as she spends increasing amounts of each week in the IT department. In most cases, the CMIO will be able to schedule her clinical time around standing IT department meetings, but the challenge will come when one-of-a-kind meetings or ad hoc IT meetings need to be scheduled on a clinical day or on an urgent basis and the CMIO already has patients waiting. The CMIO's boss will need to be tolerant of the demands and challenges of care providers. It may be more difficult to reschedule multiple patients than for a CxO's administrative assistant to reschedule a meeting. The CxO needs to realize that part of the CMIO's value to the organization comes with the continuing clinical experience and medical staff authenticity of a clinically practicing CMIO. Finally, the CMIO will need to inquire of her manager whether her clinical position brings additional salary support to her home department, additional salary income directly to the CMIO, or whether clinical time is included in the home department's CMIO salary.

CONCLUSION

The CMIO position can be very valuable to an organization. There are a wide variety of duties that the CMIO can perform based on the CMIO's experience, desires, and clinical duties, the organization's complexity and reporting structure, and the implementation status of major clinical information systems, to name a few. Depending on the CMIO's career plans, the CMIO may desire operational and budget responsibility. The CMIO needs to be aware of the various role choices, the potential risks to the organization of those options, and the areas of possible overlap and conflict with other leaders. If the CMIO goes in knowing his or her own preferences and if the CMIO is willing to engage in candid and direct discussions with his or her manager, the CMIO will be able to negotiate a successful role that will lead to happiness and effectiveness for both the CMIO and the organization.

CHAPTER 6

Authority and Power Shape the CMIO Role: Influencer, Decision Maker or Both?*

By Steven J. Davidson, MD, MBA, FACEP, FACPE, and Howard Landa, MD

The field of medical informatics has evolved far faster than has the role of the physician informaticist. As non-clinical computing grew from adding machines and ledgers to financial systems and the enterprise resource planning (ERP) systems that now underlie major healthcare organizations, clinical computing has evolved from nurses determining intravenous (IV) drip rates with hand-held calculators to our present interconnected era in which an EHR supporting CPOE is integrated through a wireless network to an infusion controller with "guardrails" intended to enhance patient safety for the administration of infused medications. Yet throughout these past decades of practical evolution in our healthcare delivery environments, physician involvement, though continuous, has been mostly marginal, but rarely central and engaged as it might have been.

---

* This chapter owes much of its structure and ideas for the content to: Dinnerman N. Political realities. In Kuehl, AE: *Prehospital Systems and Medical Oversight.* 3rd ed. National Association of EMS Physicians, Dubuque, OA: Kendall/Hunt Publishing Company; 2002.

The HITECH Act, enacted as part of the American Recovery and Reinvestment Act of 2009, was signed into law on February 17, 2009, to promote the adoption and "meaningful use" [MU] of health IT. The Patient Protection and Affordable Care Act (PPACA) is a federal statute that was signed into United States' law by President Barack Obama on March 23, 2010. This act and the Health Care and Education Reconciliation Act of 2010 (signed into law on March 30, 2010) made up the healthcare reform of 2010. Together these laws and the attendant federal financial support for EHRs have altered the landscape, requiring healthcare enterprises of all sizes to engage their physicians for much more than the occasional explanation of a clinical process (particularly those in which workflow is not yet a common term). While for some organizations, the effort to achieve MU may be little more than another revenue raiser for most, it is but the first step on the path to healthcare transformation and organizational transformation into a value-driven healthcare delivery enterprise.

While practicing physicians have historically acted mostly as consultants and influencers in clinical informatics endeavors, those physicians who aspired to spend substantial time working in the field of medical informatics have been frustrated by limited opportunities for leadership and a paucity of the skills needed in management of people and projects. Clinicians' singular focus on patient outcome and experience sometimes provoked conflict with other leaders who often felt that physicians lacked the experience and knowledge of the operations context necessary for keeping the healthcare organization's doors open and staff paid. Then too, physician compensation levels were a point of irritation; as a non-clinical IT staffer earned far less than did a physician, most organizations could not and did not desire to compensate physicians who would work in medical informatics sufficiently to compete with clinical practice. Compliance with state and federal regulations regarding paying clinicians who were not full-time employees for services to the organization also became a concern. However, more recently many organizations recognize the value of a clinician's contribution, and the evolution of descriptive terms for the role provides a metaphor for this progression: initially "DataDocs" or "CompuDocs" followed by "Physician Champions" or one author's (Howard Landa) contribution, the "Medical Informatics Gadfly."

Most recently the career of Medical Informaticist has progressed, and we now hold titles such as Director of Medical Informatics and CMIO.

While the necessity for engaged, accountable physician leadership has become clear, organizations still vary in their preparation and capacity to usefully incorporate physician leadership in medical and clinical informatics yielding diverse roles for physicians, often functioning as advisors, consultants, and influencers, even if all under the rubric of Chief Medical Information (Informatics) Officer.

Historically, pragmatic practicing physicians have responded effectively to the urgent external demands of expertise and specialty development. One of this chapter's authors participated in an earlier era of patient-demanded access and improvement to emergency services, which led to the development of the specialty of emergency medicine. Now, too, we authors of this text through a range of daily activities have been and continue to do the work on the ground required to bring the benefits of EHRs to our patients, the clinicians, and organizations that care for them, even as organized medicine at this writing is contemplating the creation of subspecialty recognition for medical informatics through the development of a curriculum and training programs. Many specialty boards have expressed interest and the possibility of certification examination availability as early as 2013, as has been reported.*

Now, however, the paradigm is changing. CMIOs are being given real responsibilities and accountabilities. The CMIO now frequently has a "seat at the table" in the boardroom and has been given the authority to manage complex projects and implementations. We are becoming actively involved in an organization's strategic planning process. Unfortunately, in many cases, we are ill-equipped for this role. Medicine tends to select for independence and self-reliant individuals, and medical training reinforces this by its apprenticeship teaching approach. People management, team play, sales and marketing acumen, and change management expertise are not skills taught in medical school. In this chapter, we hope to present insights and some

---

* Detmer DE, Munger BS, Lehmann CU: Clinical informatics board certification: History, current status, and predicted impact on the clinical informatics workforce. *Appl Clin Inf.* 2009;1:11-18 doi: 10.4338/ACI-2009-11-R-0016. Last accessed February, 2011.

simple but effective tools to move from the role of "champion" or "influencer" to the role of leader and decision maker.

The successful CMIO doesn't merely liaise between administrators and clinicians but connects the business operations of a healthcare enterprise with the clinical delivery of patient care. By implementing innovative advances in clinical care through the use of medical informatics while participating with and sometimes leading a team of clinicians and administrators, she or he as a change agent builds respect for the useful outcome, while respecting the efforts of all participants.

The CMIO recognizes that the evolving role mandates a degree of flexibility not usually associated with clinicians and requires an ability to move among various degrees of involvement, perhaps on a project-by-project basis or on a departmental or divisional basis (see Figure 6-1).

Figure 6-1. Level of involvement between the CMIO and other management partners in the medical informatics enterprise. (From Workplace Systems, Inc., 1995, as revised in 2011. Used by permission.)

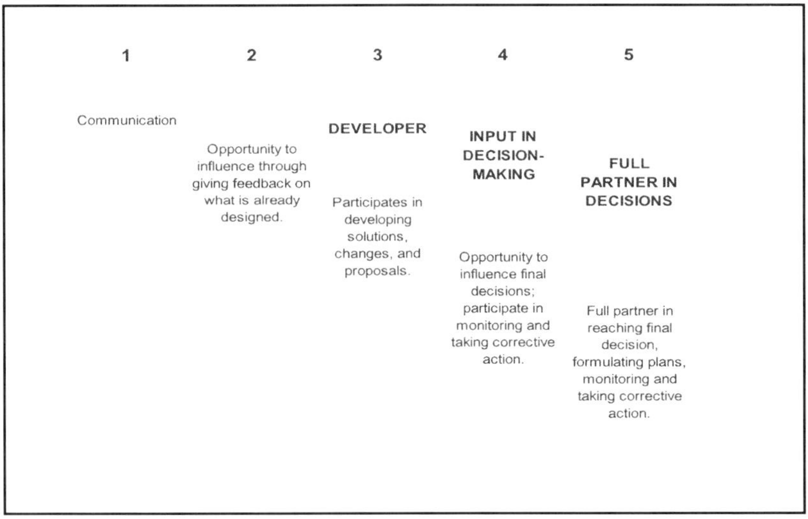

The CMIO confronts this sometimes daunting challenge depending upon his/her own creativity in a complex environment—the political arena. The multiple relationships required of the CMIO within and beyond the medical community create an especially challenging practice in which technical expertise by itself often proves insufficient to the tasks necessary for the current project or the overall mission of the medical information enterprise.

For some physicians, while the challenge is undeniably attractive, the emotional energy required and the intense ongoing interactions in the political arena may vitiate the passion of the most engaged CMIO. As with other disciplines in medicine—even life itself—an apprenticeship may be a means for conveying the skills needed in the CMIO's practice from the veteran to the neophyte. Professional associations and collegial relationships can be helpful. The organizational structure within which the CMIO works varies among organizations and are addressed in Chapter 2, Reporting Structure-Organizational Structure, but these structures provide the starting place from which the CMIO exerts political behavior toward the success of the medical information enterprise—ultimately perhaps affecting and even altering the administrative structure within which the CMIO works.

Politics and economics are omnipresent forces with which the CMIO grapples as he or she leads and communicates the medical informatics agenda of the health IT system. It's the rare CMIO for whom these forces are familiar and understood. Physicians who originally entered medicine in pursuit of the satisfaction derived from patient care rarely embrace these forces. Consequently, the CMIO confronts many opportunities for frustration and disappointment if approaching as the unwary and idealistic physician who has failed to acknowledge and master the elements of working effectively in an environment rife with the forces of politics and economics. Alternatively, those physicians who appreciate the leverage gained through an understanding of politics and economics will be rewarded by the accomplishments of their medical ISs and the opportunities for personal and professional development.

Sadly, the attempted metamorphosis of the clinician into a political "statesperson" more often than not results in his transmogrification into a political dyslexic. The technical dexterity and intellectual prowess of the physician do not readily provide the interpersonal skills and tools for triumphing in the political arena. Further, the frequently misperceived position of physicians as "superior" to other members of the healthcare team may seduce the CMIO into behaving as such with nonmedical individuals, with predictable and disastrous results. Political acumen must be forged slowly, over time, and with a mentor who nurtures the individual physician.

The physician who assumes the CMIO role, nonetheless, often holds a disaffection for politics found inherently in most healthcare providers—the physician comes to the role of CMIO as a "craftsman." As one of four "corporate types" defined by Maccoby in *The Gamesman,* the craftsman experiences perhaps the greatest disparity between the reality and the ideal.* It is most difficult for the physician CMIO to juxtapose the desired medical goals of a "perfect" medical IS with the political realities found in any healthcare enterprise: Friction between value systems surface. For most, the emotional cost produced by this paradigm discordance is high, and for some, too great to sustain a career of permanence in this aspect of practice. In the pursuit of quality, however, the craftsperson is handicapped by the lack of a definition easily communicated to the political veterans among the IT system leaders at the hospital or practice. Quality, as with style, class, and poise, tend to be attributes of human behavior which are recognizable but poorly articulated. It's the rare CMIO who comes to the role with his or her "political awareness gene" fully engaged—for most, it's been a dormant gene which must be "turned on."

While many definitions of politics abound, for the CMIO, a pragmatic definition might be, "an attempt to engender, gather, manufacture, or express consensus." The relationship of consensus to the technically ideal health IT environment may be at best oblique, from the perspective of the scientifically forged physician "craftsman." The genesis of the local health IT environment is mostly not founded on logic and rationality. Rather, economics and politics—which possess the power or the money and which "sleep" with whom—are more often the determining factors. While the CMIO may desire an arena devoid of political influences, this is as impossible to achieve as eliminating the vagaries of human behavior itself.

---

* Maccoby M. *The Gamesman: The New Corporate Leaders.* New York: Simon and Schuster; 1976.

STAKEHOLDER AGENDAS AND PRESSURE POINTS

The approach of the CMIO who is new to the role must be one of openness, and great caution. While espousing an ideal system, it is well for the physician to identify the power blocs. Typically, they consist of the following:

- The Board
- CEO
- CFO
- CMO
- CNO
- CIO
- Patients
- Physicians
- Nurses
- Corporate Counsel (attorney)
- The Joint Commission and other regulatory bodies

Fundamental to appreciating the appropriate development of the medical IS is the need for the CMIO to understand the pressure points within it. This requires patience, a willingness to invest time with each of these principles, and an ability to discern the history of the present situation. A pivotal mission for the CMIO is to reframe, refocus, and redefine the agendas of others. Clearly, he or she must become intimate with the capabilities and desires of each of the provider groups and the position of corporate leaders before attempting to choreograph development and improvement of the medical IS for the enterprise. Each of the aforementioned stakeholders has an agenda which can be viewed as a "political vector" with magnitude (force) and direction. The CMIO's objective becomes the exertion of pressure in such a way as to realign the vectors as parallel as possible toward the development, implementation, refinement, and maintenance of the desired medical information system.

MASTER THE POLITICAL "SENSES"

Five political senses require mastery:

- **A sense of mission**—Yours, that of the CMIO's leadership role, and that of the institution—should first be defined, then amalgamated and articulated. It may be helpful to frame the efforts of the CMIO not only as a practice champion and political choreographer but as a genetic engineer as well. Indeed, the manipulation of the clinical practice environment is analogous to skillfully revising— through the medical IS—the "genetic code" of the practice environment of the clinical enterprise, propagating through a management information system (MIS), the tools of clinical practice that optimize patient outcomes while supporting clinician practices. The CMIO must speak most directly to his or her mission as trustee—medical fiduciary on behalf of patients.

- **A sense of tradition**—The history of the healthcare enterprise and the clinical service within it should be studied. This provides guidance in maneuvering around the political obstacles, which have emplaced barriers toward development.
- **A sense of position**—The position of the CMIO within the enterprise must be acknowledged, particularly relationships with clinical leaders and the IT enterprise. As we saw in Figure 6-1, the CMIO may variably participate in different roles at different times. Perhaps as regards purely technical or business functions, the CMIO will be informed or consulted; systems supporting human resource functions may benefit from the CMIO as co-developer or holding input into decision making. In clinical systems, the CMIO as a full partner in decisions can serve as the preeminent leader of the health IT enterprise in formulating plans, monitoring results, and taking corrective action.
- **Humor**—As an invaluable aid to personal equanimity, team cohesion, and constructive relationships. Cultivate this skill throughout your career, and it will lengthen your professional lifespan.
- **Timing**—Watch the horizon, observe the enterprise strategic plan, and take advantage of the changes being introduced when timing the implementation of your new ideas and programs.

PREPARING ONESELF FOR THE CMIO ROLES OF INFLUENCER AND DECISION MAKER

Accomplishing the enterprise and personal mission requires achievement in five spheres: academic, operational, administrative, clinical, and human relations. The target audience for the CMIO should be defined in the broadest possible context, that of other healthcare providers—all who work in the enterprise, patients, and every other "customer" whom the CMIO touches. As just one example, recall that environmental services personnel may never "login," yet they will clean, move, and work around devices you play a role in selecting and implementing—thus, they too are part of your constituency.

Understand the concept of "Political Darwinism": The political and economic environment defines reality. As the environment changes, "carpe diem," —you must adapt or perish; in other words, "mutate or die." The CMIO whose innovative management and communication styles, whose strategic awareness keeps him/her attuned to the big picture, is the leader best able to adapt the needs of his or her enterprise to the vicissitudes of politics, Sadly, Darwinism is not pretty.

The CMIO must know and act on political principles, yet not be a politician. A politician is loyal to his or her constituency; the CMIO will be loyal to the principles of sound clinical practice. That the CMIO demonstrates awareness of the political climate in which he or she must work does not impugn his/her motives. Thus, neither should he or she apologize for his or her political insight.

Systems evolve—slowly. The CMIO's sanity will best be preserved if he or she appreciates the geological timeframes within which change may be accomplished. Organizational learning and cultural change, vendor development of systems, and skill development by clinicians may take much of a decade. One will invariably be disappointed by how little one accomplishes in a year and how much has been accomplished in a decade.

Nurture your colleagues. Patients and issues come and go. Long after your colleagues have forgotten the reason for your anger, they will recall the unpleasantness of the interaction. Expressed alternatively, friends may come and go, but enemies accumulate. Your colleagues outlast the issues, and should be respected. Technical errors are more easily forgiven than normative or behavioral errors. Strive to develop equanimity, an ethical, emotional, and behavioral steadiness within you. An even-tempered, stable operational perspective allows you to weather the vicissitudes of system change, maintaining constancy of purpose toward the vision you, your colleagues and enterprise have identified.

Always strive to create win–win solutions; when this is impossible, ensure that all participate in the necessary compromises.

Be the source and you become the force; don't strive to become the power broker. By striving to become the source, (i.e., the consultative resource to whom people turn for guidance), the CMIO becomes a powerful force for change.

Define the quality of your service in meaningful terms. Utilize sufficient measures of quality so that you can point to constraining measures for each and so that you can speak to quality in terms understood by all of your intended audiences.

Every system improvement is a political statement; so is every unscheduled downtime.

Choose realistic mentors. Mentors who are great and flawed are more likely to be emulated than those who are perceived as great and perfect. The former are seen as human, the latter, god-like. We see some hope of improving upon the former but are never able to reach the standards of the latter.

Observe why others fail. As CMIO you must have a good engine (innate talent), a good transmission (personality and communication skills), plenty of fuel in the tank (endurance), and landmarks and route signs (constructive feedback).

Develop a shared paradigm with your team. Stress the provision of services with competence, compassion, class, creativity, and credibility.

Strive to develop a demeanor and countenance which reflects an academic, intellectual, and collegial approach to solving problems. Maintain your equanimity.

A special note of caution about bureaucracies is in order— your enterprise corporate counsel may be your most challenging bureaucracy. The confrontational opponent is easy to identify if not to outmaneuver, but the bureaucrat may prove lethal to developments and improvements if for no other reason than his or her resistance to innovation, persistent adherence to process, and longevity in the role. The bureaucracy can consume enormous amounts of the CMIO's energy. More reforms have been defeated in an attempt to navigate a bureaucratic quagmire than the withering verbal artillery of individual or collective opponents. Bureaucrats fundamentally perceive themselves as underappreciated, if not powerless. A bureaucrat, if provoked, can erect enormous obstacles and subvert and condemn the most noble and meritorious ideas of the CMIO, if only to demonstrate his power over the physician. Respect, acknowledgement, and interaction with the bureaucracy may not provide a dramatic victory but it will pave the way for one.

PRINCIPLES OF ACTION

Medical informatics leadership is inextricably tethered to hospital healthcare politics and economics. Every system implementation and unanticipated downtime is thus a political, and an economic statement. Institutional paranoia dictates that whoever controls the ISs controls the data and the revenue. Into this economic maelstrom is placed the CMIO for whom none of this fiscal agenda is inherently germane, but in which the service he is to provide exists. Is it any wonder that as CMIO this foreign political and economic environment feels hostile? Adhering to an evidence-based course can become a daunting ordeal.

In this inherently unfamiliar arena, certain principles empower the CMIO for greater probability of success:

Master political judo. As with its physical counterpart, the politically diminutive physician—empowered by his allegiance to principles of medicine—understands the maneuvers necessary to tumble opponents in the desired direction. Having no need to serve a political constituency or react to the egomaniacal forces of his opponents, the CMIO is more effective exploiting their psychopathology than perseverating about it.

Before pushing the first domino, know where the last one falls. Do not be tempted by the seductively easy "win," unless you are aware of all the political connections of your opponents. Better to be one who sets up the dominoes than the one who pushes them. Natural political forces will cause one to fall eventually. The wise CMIO will have spent years establishing the desired direction in which the dominoes should fall, content that fate or circumstance will eventually tumble the first one.

The movements of a chess game are instructive. The pawn, slowly moving ahead, can become as effective as any other chess piece. At any time, the chessboard can be upset, moving all the pieces in different and unpredictable directions: vendors merge, regulators alter priorities, hospital administrators move on. A strategic leader acquires a global perspective of each piece on the chessboard. Consistent performance over time will usually create substantial success.

Covet identified problems. Complaints may be seen as "opportunities in drag." They permit creative manipulation of the system and insight into behavioral issues, which must be addressed. The CMIO is a problem solver, as much as any other single role he or she plays.

Identify the relationships among people throughout your enterprise. Your enterprise is a complex political eco-system, with myriad political connections among even the most far-flung members. A movement or alteration of the power anywhere in your environment may affect others elsewhere. For example, interactions among primarily outpatient and inpatient clinicians who care for the same patients may be seriously altered by political and economic decisions that affect leadership in the laboratory or radiology.

Become dispensable, but not openly so. As a wise physician administrator once demonstrated, place your finger in the middle of a glass of water. The finger represents your presence within your enterprise. Remove your finger. Notice the hole that is left.

Learn to swim with sharks. Thus, if bitten, do not bleed. Before recognizing another individual as a non-shark, ensure that you have witnessed docile behavior on more than one occasion.

Rescue an injured swimmer with due regard for external and internal reasons for his incapacity, lest you succumb during the effort. Periodically give a known shark a forceful punch in the nose to remind him that you have some power.

Stage a crisis on your own terms. When a crisis looms, ensure that you orchestrate it to occur at such time that it will be optimal for you. For example, if confronting a capital budget that omits a system update, ally yourself with medical staff leadership who has a particular interest in that system. Work with these leaders to focus attention on the urgency for the update at the moment when administrators or board members' attention can be drawn to the issue because of relevant industry or political news.

Be a political chameleon. It is helpful to have a full set of costumes to enable you to project a panoply of images, appropriate to the political moment.

Identify all the customers. Too frequently, only the patient is identified as the customer. Within any organization, however, internal and external customers must be satisfied. They are not necessarily direct supervisors of the CMIO. Every individual within the system who must be satisfied, or at least acknowledged, should be identified, and never ignored.

Understand what business you are really in. As CMIO, you are a key leader supporting the systems supporting care. Your challenge is to rise above the image of the physician as a provider of care to individual patients. In providing the clinical leadership for the entire medical IS, you care for thousands of people and influence the well-being of people far beyond the limits of a single individual. This becomes one of the strongest motivating factors for the craftsman to continue the quest for system improvement.

Project academic passion with political neutrality. Manifest your allegiance to medical imperatives; keep patients and the families and communities from whence they come at the center of your focus, while supporting the work of your clinical colleagues and maintaining your political equanimity.

Visible power is vulnerable power. The final decision maker enjoys the most ego-gratification and the least potential for long-term survival. The individual who is invisible and informal in the use of power is most insulated from assault but will not enjoy adoration of the public or wide recognition in an organization. Strive for a position between these two extremes; seek a "low profile" but a formal authority, which enables your role and achieving a personal power base.

Never satisfy a bureaucratic need completely. To do so will cause them to forget you. Partial solution enables an occasional reminder to the bureaucracy of your importance as a problem solver, and your inadequate funding.

Control many key factors but not all. For example, the CMIO must retain responsibility for convening and communicating with the medical staff and bringing this sometimes fractious group to consensus while simultaneously supporting the medical staff leadership when their clinical priorities differ from administrative direction. Participate in clinical support system decisions—you must participate in decisions regarding the online telephone directory, widely used by the medical staff; however, there will be systems in which you need not play a role.

Avoid the use of fear, embarrassment, anger, frustration, intimidation, and guilt. These are transparent and managerially myopic means of motivating behavior. They are also anti-academic, anti-intellectual, and anti-collegial.

Survival alone defines a certain success of design and merits your respect. Individuals who have existed within your organization for some time have evolved successful forms of adaptation. Do not ignore what may appear to be conservative postures, or clever camouflage.

Remain vigilant, but not suspicious. The latter is an emotionally draining posture with which to confront life.

SUBJECT PROJECTS TO THE OREO ANALYSIS

- Identify Opportunities

- Identify Resources
- Identify Expectations
- Identify Obstructions

FOLLOWING THROUGH AND SUMMARY

History belongs to the person of letters, the student of language, but most of all to the master of synthesis. The CMIO who can amalgamate the owned and voluntary resources of his or her healthcare enterprise contributes inestimable value to his/her community of care. Remember that institutions, professions, and communities are platforms for your creativity. Respect them, engage them, and ensure that they are used wisely.

Each CMIO must consider his or her own personal evolution. Leverage your creativity at every opportunity. Assist not only a limited population of patients but your entire community. In the process, contribute to the knowledge base of the specialty and assist an entire nation. Key to this personal evolution is the need to become "more than a physician" as CMIO.

To this end, the CMIO should consider acquiring the knowledge, skills, and abilities from other professions such as teaching and business, to augment his or her own innate talent. Such education may be acquired by either informal (apprenticeship) or formal (MBA acquisition) methods. Borrowing from other professions to augment the persuasive talents of the physician can be extremely powerful. Likewise, adding non-medical literature, such as the *Harvard Business Review* and the *Wall Street Journal,* will suggest a multitude of approaches, which are effective in the political and economic venues of the enterprise in which the CMIO must secure his or her vision.

Identify your own vision as CMIO, so as to remain professionally satisfied by performing meaningful work, identifying and placing yourself proximate to role models to emulate, and keep things eclectic. Have fun by trying to capture a childhood fantasy every day. Contribute substantively; figureheads soon become hood ornaments, and the first to be sacrificed when systems crash.

Yet, always have an exit strategy for yourself. The frustration of negotiation among those with competing interests over the years may be lessened by identifying the myriad other venues in which your creativity can be expressed. When your effectiveness has waned, and your tenure is drawing to a close, a timely, gracious, and dignified exit will nullify the harshest critics and establish your accomplishments in institutional memory.

CHAPTER 7

Following on a Success or Failure: What's Next for the CMIO?

By Jerome Wang, MD, FAAP, FACP

Especially in recent years, examples of successful large-scale, organization-wide clinical IS implementation can more easily be found. From these organizations, it is clear that strong physician informatics leadership is a critical component in successfully bridging the gap between technology and clinical practice. As discussed in previous chapters, the early typical role of the physician leader in "early-adopter" institutions was that of a physician "engineer." Charged with bringing clinical ISs into clinical practice, these physician leaders bridged the capabilities and constraints of the IT with the clinical processes that could be impacted by these systems and redesigned these processes to benefit most from the technology. Some of these early pioneers worked with either home-grown or early commercial systems in co-development partnerships with vendors and quickly learned that risky clinical and political disruption caused by immature technology could be minimized by small tweaks in the technology to fit the local workflow.

Although avoiding tumultuous change on a large scale helped protect the technology from sheer rejection, the numerous cycles of technical change, followed by retraining and re-implementation, easily expanded the timeline and overall organizational cost to achieve technology-enabled clinical change. The more significant the clinical and technical disruption, the more complex and challenging the change management on all levels: clinical, technical, and political. Healthcare executives began to realize that large-scale technology implementation, although more risky, also had the potential for more rapid and widespread impact. Simply put, no pain, no gain. The picture of clinical transformation founded on IT began to emerge as much of an organizational change as much as a technical one. And as the number of viable vendor-based clinical ISs increased, so did the number of organizations with an appetite for broad IT-enabled clinical transformation.

As discussed in previous chapters, the role of the CMIO has evolved in line with this organizational need. Now, not only is physician leadership needed to precisely marry technology, content, and workflow, but the CMIO is also tasked with responsibility at the executive level to help direct and move the organization along the path toward IT-enabled transformation. Clearly, many organizations have identified the role of the CMIO as an important figure in this regard, but is it the CMIO who carries primary responsibility for overcoming the key organizational barriers that threaten eventual success? How will success (or failure) be measured, and how can the new CMIO remain accountable, yet avoid unfair expectations or blame?

THE RISK OF SUCCESS OR FAILURE

Organizations looking for a CMIO must candidly and openly evaluate the gaps that they are looking for the CMIO candidate to fill, as the candidate must simultaneously consider not only the published job description but the in-between-the-lines expectations and competencies of those working around him or her. The CMIO must address these issues early, as the success of this role is tightly coupled to the overall success of the clinical IT initiative and beyond.

Three critical pillars (see Figure 7-1) upholding (or undermining) the success of a large-scale clinical IT transformation initiative can be conceptually grouped into three different codependent stacks:
  • Organizational readiness and clinician alignment;
  • Project management and execution; and

- Technical performance and clinical integration

And while it is unusual for the CMIO to be wholly administratively responsible for any of these pillars, one could argue that one of the most important responsibilities of the CMIO is to horizontally bind these vertical pillars, to bolster organizational integration as a political, administrative, and clinical leader who can anticipate, communicate, and facilitate the cultural, technical, and clinical changes that will occur across traditional organizational lines. That is not to say that the direct responsibilities of the CMIO are insignificant or lack accountability for any of these roles, but rather that the CMIO's success is extremely dependent on his or her ability to foster a broad level of support from physician leadership and executive management within and across these foundational pillars.

Figure 7-1. Organizational transformation with clinical information technology

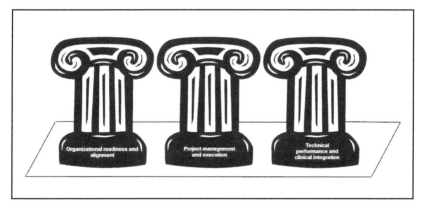

In this regard, what are the reporting and functional relationships of the CMIO with the project, executive management, and medical staff leadership? This is discussed more formally in other chapters dedicated to the CMIO's key relationships (especially Chapter 4: What Is the CMIO's Relationship with the Medical Staff), but suffice it to say, consistent communication and deep trust among the organizational leaders is a must. A fundamental breakdown of communication or misalignment along any of the key management lines has the potential to handicap the IT implementation, clinician adoption, and/or its expected business or clinical goals. Because of this inherent dependency on others and the tight association of the CMIO role to a large IT-capital initiative, the unsuspecting CMIO could be seen as an easy target for blame in the case of a significant IT failure. However, the failures that occur are often a combination of organizational, project execution, and technical factors that lie above and beyond the CMIO's areas of direct line responsibility. Yet the CMIO has an opportunity to significantly guide decisions and significantly influence the course of the initiative based on the breadth of his or her background and depth of relationships. The CMIO should be viewed as a necessary but not a sufficient executive to help support and manage the clinical, technical, and organizational changes.

WHAT'S NEXT AFTER AN IT FAILURE OR SUCCESS?

Not surprisingly, we all love success stories, and this is no different in regards to healthcare IT. As more organizations step forward to share their healthcare IT triumphs, it is easy to point out key factors in achieving this success. For those successful organizations boasting of a CMIO, the importance of the CMIO role is hoisted in the organizational afterglow of success, while difficulties, non-fatal missteps, and temporary regrets are forgotten in the thrill of victory. The portrait of the successful CMIO emerges as one of an organizational catalyst, one with a horizontal understanding of technology, clinical process improvement, local organizational culture and politics, and the humble leadership qualities needed to broadly engage and disarm physicians, nurses, and management. The contribution of the other key executives is likewise idealized. When a clinical IT initiative does well, everyone wins, and the typically exhausted organization can bask for at least a short moment. Success is a team effort.

But what happens when a significant clinical IT investment is considered a less-than-success or perhaps an outright failure? Anecdotes of less-than-successful implementations are probably more widespread (and much less publicized) than many are willing to admit, and few are willing to step forward to share the responsibility. In the root-cause-analysis phase of a clinical IT initiative gone wrong, one must ask: What was the role of the CMIO? What is he or she accountable for? One could evaluate a given CMIO against her published job description and direct areas of line authority, but as discussed already, the role of the CMIO is precariously balanced on a variety of external factors and peers to achieve true success in this leadership position. She must be effective as a communicator, negotiator, politician, and leverage her clinical credibility, integrity, and relationships to build trust with organizational leaders and influencers. The ability to leverage these intangibles to successfully deliver tangible results are what ultimately should be the measure of success or failure of the CMIO, regardless of the written job description.

To give a more practical example, most CMIOs will oversee the development of clinical content, including documentation templates, clinical decision-support and order sets and their integration into the clinical workflow. The experience of many large EHR implementations is that the clinical content can significantly influence whether physician users perceive the system as intuitive or clinically "smart." It is one of the critical factors in either fostering physician adoption or provoking physician resistance. If the content is clinically inadequate to improve clinical care or doesn't facilitate workflow and EHR adoption, then the CMIO should rightly be considered responsible, right? Perhaps, but unfortunately, it is never that simple.

For example, a CMIO at a large academic hospital may assemble a number of workgroups to create EHR-based clinical order sets and documentation tools. For the department of cardiology, the workgroup members include a practicing community cardiologist, a pharmacist, the clinical chief, and a cardiovascular physician researcher. The well-respected cardiology investigator is shortly looking to enroll patients in an NIH-funded clinical trial and is very interested in harnessing the EHR to identify patients eligible for enrollment in this study. He is hoping that the implementation of inpatient clinical documentation will help him capture enrollment criteria at the point-of-care and help his long-standing struggle to recruit subjects for clinical trials, and so he volunteers to work with the implementation team to development templates. But it becomes apparent that the content being proposed is biasing the documentation templates into more of a research enrollment form than a clinical tool that cardiologists or internists would use during a hospital admission. He would like for the EHR team to mandate use of the template and the capture of key study enrollment criteria.

In addition, the clinical chief of cardiology has been working with the CQO in a struggle to remind physicians to assess left ventricular ejection fraction (LVEF) when a patient is admitted for congestive heart failure (CHF) in response to The Joint Commission's core measures around heart failure. The hospital has been struggling to improve adherence rates, and the clinical chief would like to implement a number of non-specific pop-up alerts early with hospital EHR implementation to remind the admitting physician to order an echocardiogram if not done recently.

The pharmacist participating in this workgroup reviews the medications and suggests that the CPOE order set for CHF include only ramipril, which is the preferred angiotensin-converting enzyme (ACE) inhibitor on formulary, whereas the current paper process allows a physician to order any ACE inhibitor, which then requires the pharmacist to auto-substitute the medication with an equivalent dose of a formulary drug. He is hoping that this change in prescribing options would reduce the extra work of the pharmacy department in performing auto-substitutions.

The community cardiologist on the workgroup doesn't use ramipril and is adamant that the EHR should not force him and others to change their practice and prescribe a medication with which they aren't familiar. He strongly opposes the idea that an admitting cardiologist or hospitalist should be mandated to enter CHF study enrollment criteria and further states that any competent cardiologist wouldn't fail to assess LVEF. He is weary of the EHR wielding "big-brother" alerts and feels that other community physicians who admit to the hospital will see the alerts as obtrusive.

In this vignette, most experienced readers would agree that these views are more than hypothetical and that any one of the viewpoints, if left broadly unchecked across the project, could significantly hamstring the EHR initiative. Physicians could react negatively by premature and overzealous use of alerts. Well-meaning but uninformed stakeholders may attempt to bundle "special-interest" changes in clinical practice with initial EHR implementation, without patiently waiting for the acceptance phase to reach a stable and sustainable level. On the other hand, if the organization ignores the need for key areas of standardization and fails to adequately build a foundation of policies and tactical decisions toward leveraging the EHR for quality and research, the organization may ultimately find itself with a used but also a fractionally potent tool.

So, the underlying storyline is that the CMIO and his team not only have a real challenge to engage a broad swath of clinical experts and stakeholders to contribute their efforts and buy-in to the initiative but must also skillfully and proactively establish governance policies and processes that will help steer the project away from avoidable hazards. At the same time, the CMIO and his other leadership partners must skillfully negotiate consensus-driven decision making in light of these policies, without disenfranchising the zealous stakeholder. Success or failure, the CMIO should clearly be judged on tangible work product for a large system initiative, but his evaluators must understand that this product is but a culmination of how successfully the CMIO can cultivate engagement of key organizational stakeholders, drive proactive policies in anticipation of project hazards, skillfully manage passionate but widely differing viewpoints with skill, and disarm the most vocal naysayer with gentleness and calm.

It is this set of translational skills, coupled with a thick skin and a pervasive determination that the CMIO brings to the executive roundtable, the ability to facilitate physician engagement, catalyze decision making with a high view of consensus, and bridge clinical processes with technology in light of a horizontal understanding of organizational policy, clinical change management, and technology-based transformation. Regardless of the organization's ultimate declaration of success or failure, the CMIO should be measured by a combination of tangible work-product and less tangible administrative and organizational skills but also viewed as a highly dependent role, enabled only by a supportive cadre of organizational leaders demonstrating a spirit of collaboration and credible technical and project execution. A CMIO is best viewed as a necessary but not independently sufficient role to help an organization succeed in technology-enabled clinical transformation.

As previously discussed, the CMIO has evolved out of a need for a multifaceted clinical leadership in anticipation of and during large organizational clinical IT projects. As other chapters in this book more formally describe the role of the CMIO, qualitatively one would observe that most job descriptions tie the role of the CMIO to the initial goal of achieving successful implementation and technology-driven clinical changes. Although some organizations will continue to invest in new areas of clinical information implementation, most organizations are bounded by limited resources and necessarily turn their attention to post-implementation tasks. This phase focuses on leveraging the IT investment to achieve financial goals, underwrite business strategy, or demonstrate impact on clinical quality or efficiency. As the institution moves toward this post-implementation phase, many who assumed the original rationale for hiring a CMIO was primarily tied to implementation, might ask, "What's next after the 'project' is over? What is the function of the now veteran CMIO?"

Perhaps a seasoned CMIO may realize that an idealistic measure of success is for his original job description to become outdated. An organization successfully nurtured in part by the CMIO through a large-scale EHR initiative begins to speak and function in a new reality. Terms such as clinical content and workflow analysis, once considered unintelligible jargon, become common vernacular among management and clinicians. Physicians and nurses begin to use the technology in a very efficient manner, no longer moving awkwardly through newly designed clinical care processes, and become accustomed to working in an environment made transparent by IT. End-users' questions begin to become more sophisticated, and clinicians begin to demonstrate a higher comfort and willingness to work toward consensus decisions independently. Although the CMIO now has a battle-proven set of skills and experience, the now maturing organization will look to benefit from these skills in a different way.

Hopefully, with proper planning and budgeting, the successful post-implementation organization is able to shift into a lower intensity but equally as important phase of optimization, with the realization that although the implementation was successful, the process of leveraging its IT investment to achieve organization goals is a work that has just begun. At first, the optimization efforts may include remaining priority fixes to technology or processes (or both), but soon inconspicuously morph from "fixes" into "enhancement" priorities that involve changes in the clinical care process, operations, and clinical staff behavior more than significant technology changes. The CMIO, with a broad understanding of the clinical, workflow, and political landscape, can play an important leadership role in this regard and helps to reframe the existing governance and oversight groups to participate in this process, but in many organizations, then turns his attention to leveraging the stability of the tool to target clinical quality and efficiency targets. Indeed, in a recent (2007) Gartner survey, a quarter of CMIO respondents considered their organizations in an IT lifecycle that was ripe for them to assume an increased role in quality measurement and the use of IT to drive quality and process improvement.

Depending on the organization and the scope of the original initiative, there may be opportunities for new IT-based projects, such as clinical information system extension into new clinical care settings (i.e., ambulatory EMR, patient-provider Web-portal, etc.) and connecting the newly installed EHR to the community (i.e, PHRs, RHIO activities, etc.). This is perhaps enough to keep a CMIO perpetually engaged in clinical transformation efforts. In addition, given the ever-changing landscape of health IT, many organizations have historically embarked on major technology conversions to replace legacy systems every 10 to 20 years. Granted, these systems have historically been largely non-clinical, but perhaps even in the current era of ever-expanding use of health IT at the point-of-care, the replacement cycle may continue to offer new challenges.

The aforementioned function of a CMIO to reach horizontally across traditional clinical, IT, and administrative lines (see Figure 7-1), also offers the opportunity to more deeply develop and test the CMIO's skills in the areas of organizational leadership, project and technical administration, and clinical quality and process improvement. So what is the natural evolution of the CMIO position with regard to other organizational roles? This may be too early to tell, but anecdotally a number of experienced CMIOs have begun to migrate into CQO, CMO, and CIO positions in their or other organizations. But regardless of whether the CMIO decides to remain in this role as a bridge between clinical practice, technology, and organizational change, it is clear that the seasoned CMIO will undoubtedly be an indelible and valuable partner in any organization seeking to transform clinical care through health IT.

CHAPTER 8

Role and Importance of the Organization's Strategic Plan

By Brian R. Jacobs, MD

As organizations focus on becoming top-tiered, there is often an accompanying recognition that technology and informatics are critical components to achieving this vision. The organizational strategic plan is often put in place and revised on an annual basis. However, what most organizations lack is an informatics and technology strategic plan that is aligned with the institutional strategic plan. The objective in developing such a complimentary approach is to focus on the automation needs for the various essential components of the organizational strategic plan. These components may include clinical care delivery, research, education, community physician relationships, patient access, and financial functions. The strategic plan should help the organization highlight the areas which will allow them to achieve best practices. Finally, it is essential that the informatics and technology strategic plan include an assessment of the technology infrastructure and architecture to ensure its strength, flexibility, and scalability for current and future growth opportunities.

The informatics and technology strategic plan should focus on defining the immediate and long-term environment from the perspective of the various enterprise stakeholders (administration, physicians, nurses, ancillary healthcare providers, staff, students, researchers, patients, and families). The plan should help to identify and focus specific goals that the organization intends to support or achieve. This vision must be balanced against the realities of the technical limitations, regulatory climate, marketplace, current best practice and competition, cultural needs, financial constraints and risks, as the planning process moves forward.

Developing an informatics and technology strategic plan for an organization requires a significant amount of work. Data need to be extracted, reviewed, and analyzed; recent organizational and IT strategic plans need to be studied; focus groups representing all organizational interests need to be conducted; while industry and competition require investigation. The plan may be conducted using internal resources, external consultants, or both. Internal resources must be allocated dedicated time to participate in the plan. For this reason, if internal resources or expertise are limited in strategic planning, some organizations choose to outsource the effort to an effective consultant. It is important to note that even if the work is outsourced, significant internal resources will still be required for participation in focus group and validation exercises. Ultimately, if the work is performed effectively, the result will not only be the resulting multi-page strategic document, but more importantly, an effective and consolidated understanding of where the organization resides and where it needs to evolve, from an informatics and technology standpoint.

BASELINE ORGANIZATIONAL ASSESSMENT

An effective informatics and technology strategic plan should begin with a baseline organizational assessment.

1. **Assessment of Organization, People, and Services:** People are the most valuable commodity in any organization. Establishing the number of current employees, their skill sets and competencies in informatics and technology is an important first step. In many organizations employees may not be located in one area but scattered throughout engineering, IT, research, biomedical engineering, the laboratory, radiology, clinical divisions and departments, medical records, etc. There may be significant

deficiencies in coverage, as well as redundancies. The initial assessment should be focused on determining this distribution of skill sets, as well as comparing the organization to industry benchmarks to other companies of similar size and function. In addition, it will be important early on to determine whether the current informatics and technology employee numbers and function are sufficient to support current needs, as well as those for the future.

2. **Assessment of Organizational Governance, Control, and Processes:** Another essential first step is determining how informatics and technology decisions are currently made within the organization. This assessment should attempt to answer the following questions:

   a. Is the current informatics and technology governance structure and processes effective in ensuring that decisions are made with broad consensus, in an unbiased fashion and in a timely and transparent manner?

   b. Do informatics and technology decisions support the overall organizational strategy?

   c. Does informatics and technology support all of the organization's functions?

3. **Assessment of Applications Which Are Deployed and Functional:** An important component of the initial assessment includes accounting for all applications that are deployed across the organization. Each application should be assessed for the working version which is deployed and whether or not newer releases are available. An evaluation should be undertaken as to whether the application meets current and future requirements, as well as contemporary regulatory requirements.

4. **Assessment of Architecture and Technical Infrastructure:** It is not unusual for an organization to have grown beyond the capacity of its infrastructure, and therefore this must be assessed in any informatics and technology strategic plan. Specifically, it needs to be determined whether the infrastructure is able to meet current and future internal and external connectivity needs. In addition, the assessment should determine whether security and confidentiality needs are being satisfactorily addressed. The initial

assessment should determine what infrastructure enhancements are needed to optimize the use of current technology and whether the current infrastructure can support the organization's future strategies.

5. **Assessment of the Budget:** Strategic planning must take into account the current organizational annual expenditures on informatics and technology and how this compares with industry standards. The operational IT spending should be assessed as a percentage of operating budget. In addition, the capital IT spending should be evaluated as a percent of the capital budget. When framed in this way, these expenditures can be compared to national surveys by the College of Health Information Management Executives (CHIME), the Gartner group, HIMSS Analytics and other national indices. Once these financials are understood, the figures can be used to understand how much should be spent annually in the support of current and future informatics and technology needs.

6. **Assessment of the External Environment:** In order to frame the organizational strategy most effectively, it is vital to investigate current healthcare industry informatics, and technology capabilities and standards. Technology advances rapidly, and it is important to assess how technology advances, national initiatives, regulations, and other factors impact the organization. In addition, a comparison of the organization to industry benchmarks, regional competition, and national peer organizations is essential to planning efforts.

7. **Assessment of the Organizational Strategic Plan and Its Pillars:** The informatics and technology strategic plan should not exist independently from the organizational strategic plan, mission/ pillars, vision, and goals. Rather, the informatics and technology strategic plan should be closely aligned with these entities. Therefore, these organizationwide objectives should be studied closely prior to launching informatics and technology strategic planning.

8. **Assessment of the Information Technology Strategic Plan (If One Exists):** Although the informatics and technology strategic plan may be a new entity for the organization, most have had an

information technology strategic planning process in place for many years. As IT becomes more integrated into the care delivery system, education, and research, the strategic plan must do the same or risk becoming isolated. A thorough review of the existing IT strategic plan will likely yield important information useful in developing the technical and infrastructural components of the informatics and technology strategic plan.

ESTABLISHING A VISION, STRATEGIC GOALS, AND INITIATIVES

After establishing a baseline assessment, appropriate time should be devoted to the establishment of an organizational informatics and technology vision. As mentioned earlier, this vision should be closely aligned with global organizational strategy and will set the tone for the informatics and technology strategic planning process. As an example, at Children's National Medical Center in Washington, DC, the following vision has been established:

Informatics and technology supports the strategic goals of Children's National Medical Center in driving the organization to a world-class level and achieving top-tier status as a comprehensive pediatric academic institution.

This vision statement was then broken down into 10 strategic goals:

1. *High-Quality Safe Care: Supporting caregivers in the provision of high quality, safe patient care facilitated by the efficient collection of data, access to complete patient information, timely communication, availability of clinical decision support tools and evidence-based knowledge sources, and continuous monitoring and improvement.*

2. *Empowered Patients and Families: Providing highly accessible, user-friendly services, appropriate and timely communication and educational opportunities that attract and empower patients and their families as active participants in their care.*

3. *Community Health: Allowing appropriate clinical information to cross traditional organizational boundaries, resulting in the provision of the most appropriate and effective care.*

4. Broad Reach: *Enabling individuals outside the walls of the organization to participate in the exchange of ideas, educational venues, and care coordination.*

5. Data-Driven Decision Making: *Enabling the availability of all clinical administrative and financial data for timely decision making, outcomes management, research, education, financial planning, and quality improvement activities.*

6. Advocacy: *Utilizing informatics and technology to inform the development of child health policy and to support the requisite programs and education to support patient advocacy.*

7. Research: *To provide the tools and services necessary to support discovery and advance the treatment of childhood disease, while enabling the provision of integrated clinical care and research.*

8. Education: *To create a digital world for the pursuit of knowledge that supports the development of the next generation of pediatricians and presents life-long learning opportunities.*

9. Employer of Choice: *Utilizing technology to create an efficient, effective, and user-friendly organization that attracts and retains exceptional clinicians and staff.*

10. Financial Strength: *To support rigorous and robust financial planning through analysis and reporting, facilitation of optimal billing and collections, enabling performance monitoring to ensure the continued financial health of the organization.*

DATA GATHERING SESSIONS

After establishing a vision, the next step in the informatics and technology strategic planning process includes extensive data gathering sessions with important stakeholders in the organization. These stakeholders should represent a broad view of the organization from bedside care providers to the CEO and board members. Data gathering sessions are best accomplished by selecting important stakeholders with a focused agenda, a moderator, and an individual to take minutes and/or record the session. Examples include access to care, prescribing safety, remote conferencing, asset tracking, clinical documentation, etc. Data gathering sessions should focus on current strengths and weaknesses as well as future vision. For a large organization, it would not be unusual to conduct 20 to 30 such group data gathering sessions. In addition to these group sessions, individual sessions should be held with important leaders in the organization including the CEO, board members, CIO, CMIO, COO, VP of Nursing, and the CMO.

CONDUCTING A GAP ANALYSIS

Once the data gathering sessions have been completed and the results summarized, the most important next step is to conduct a gap analysis between the current state and the future ideal position. Framing these gaps in terms of the strategic goals listed earlier, as well as pointed initiatives which derive from these goals can be very helpful in aligning the strategic planning process. Each strategic initiative should be investigated in terms of its strategic priority, risk to the organization in addressing (or not addressing) the initiative, and the costs associated with addressing the initiative. Table 8-1 illustrates such a categorization of strategic gap initiatives.

Table 8-1. Sample gap analysis comparing desired to actual state for each initiative.*

Gap	Strategic Priority	Risk	Cost
Ambulatory EHR not in place	High	Moderate	High
Pharmacy information system not interoperable with CPOE	High	Moderate	Moderate
PACS images not retrievable in inpatient EHR	Moderate	Low	Low
Electronic medication reconciliation does not exist within the EHR	Moderate	Moderate	Moderate

*Each gap is categorized by strategic priority, organizational risk, and cost.

PRIORITIZING STRATEGIC INITIATIVES

After completing the gap analysis, an organization will have outlined dozens of existing informatics and technology gaps and initiatives. The prioritization of the strategic initiatives aimed at addressing these gaps may present a daunting challenge. Scoring systems can be adopted or created to place objective criteria to the issues of strategic priority, risk, and cost. An example of such a scoring system is shown in Figure 8-1. After each initiative is prioritized, the organization can then proceed in establishing specific resources required and timelines for each project.

Figure 8-1. Example of a scoring system which may be used for prioritizing initiatives.

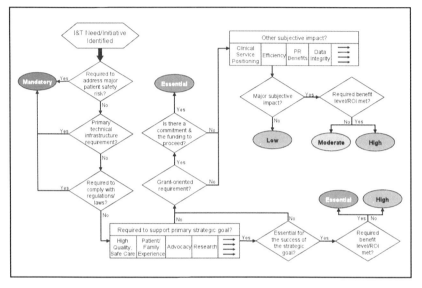

ESTABLISHING INFORMATICS AND TECHNOLOGY PRINCIPLES

In order to ensure success, any strategic plan must establish organizational principles. These principles could include:

1. Appropriate informatics and technology oversight: Ensuring that informatics and technology are deployed in a coordinated and equitable manner considering the needs of all stakeholders, strategic priorities, and resources. Customer expectations should be realistically set, decisions should be transparent, and communication should occur regularly. Customer service should be achieved in a consistent, timely, and effective manner.

2. Appropriate technology should be sought to enable the organizational strategic initiatives.

3. Securing real-time access to information should be a high priority.

4. Information sources should be integrated.

5. Technology should be implemented in a cost effective manner consistent with available resources.

6. Standardized vocabulary and data elements, common systems, and consistent policies and procedures should be adopted across the organization.

7. Systems should be maximally available to minimize downtime and disruption.

8. Applicable privacy, security, and compliance laws and regulatory agency requirements must be met.

9. Appropriate resources should be recruited and retained to support the mission and vision.

10. Consistent methodologies should be utilized in system selection, design, implementation, project management, education, and support.

11. Communication should be clear and occur on a regular basis regarding strategy, project plans, outcomes, and return on investment (ROI).

ESTABLISHING THE INFORMATICS AND TECHNOLOGY STRATEGIC FRAMEWORK

The informatics and technology strategic plan must be compatible with multiple organizational and external factors (Figure 8-2).

1. **Marketplace Availability** – Informatics and technology growth must consider the changes occurring external to the organization in industry, standards, and legislation to identify early those changes which will be required to optimize the organizational environment.

2. **Risk Tolerance** – Another important component for organizational strategy includes an assessment of the organization's tolerance for risk. Organizations are repeatedly offered new technology by both core and peripheral vendors. Much of this technology may not be ready for prime time. The strategy should consider whether the organization fits best in

the category of early, mainstream, or late technology adoption in assessing its tolerance of risk.

Figure 8-2. Example of an established framework, which is aligned with organizational strategy.

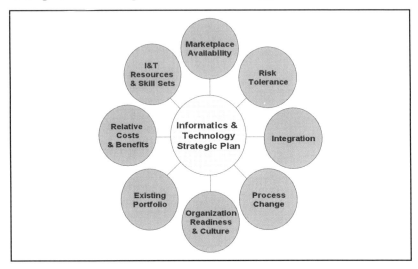

3. Integration – The framework needs to consider the organizational fit for each informatics and technology project. A general principle would likely include the adoption of a more integrated application environment over time. This means limiting stand-alone systems as a general principle, allowing best-of-breed applications only as an exception. In addition, the strategic plan should consider the need to integrate existing best-of-breed applications with other organizational ISs. Finally, strategy requires the application of interoperability standards current for industry and the organization. In addition, the human-computer interface needs to be optimized to enable most effective use of the existing and new technology.

4. Process Change – Change needs to be managed wisely in any organization. Change also requires optimal communication and education to all stakeholders. It is important to develop policies of openness, data sharing, transparency, and change management. Transitioning from a best-of-breed to an enterprise-wide approach can be a true strategic challenge as niche systems often fulfill a department's functional needs better than a solution focusing on a system-wide approach.

5. **Organizational Readiness and Culture** – When establishing the timelines of multiple projects, the informatics and technology strategic framework should consider the time necessary for organizational cultural change and stability to take place in the sequential adoption of new technologies.

6. **Existing Portfolios** – A successful informatics and technology strategic framework will need to strongly consider leveraging existing investments before moving forward. In addition, replacement of end-of-life technology at the appropriate points in time will need to be factored into the strategy. Furthermore, growth needs to be consistent with current organizational policies and procedures around security, confidentiality, and compliance. A strategy to examine core software and hardware components for required upgrades are essential to allow the organization to remain current.

7. **Relative Costs, Timelines, and Priorities** – Once a determination has been made, the informatics and technology strategic initiatives should be summarized in terms of priority, cost, and timeline. This information is best displayed graphically in a format that can be reviewed and revised on a regular basis. An example of a working document can be seen in Figure 8-3.

8. **Informatics and Technology Resources and Skill Sets** – The strategic plan should limit the number of major informatics and technology initiatives underway at any given time. Major projects must be aligned. It must also consider the organization's capacity for change. An important principle must address the organization's ability to absorb the total cost of ownership, including ongoing support for existing projects.

ESTABLISHING APPROPRIATE GOVERNANCE FOR THE ORGANIZATION

An important step in informatics and technology strategic planning includes a thorough evaluation and if needed, revision of the processes by which the organization oversees and directs informatics and technology functions. These functions must reflect and support both strategic and operational initiatives. The structure, membership, and interrelationships of the individuals making up the informatics and technology governance moving forward must be established. The governance process needs to ensure that all organizational entities are being adequately addressed and represented in the membership. In addition, it is important to establish guiding principles and an appropriate prioritization methodology for the myriad of organizational initiatives which will come to the attention of the informatics and technology governance body.

Figure 8-3: Priority, capital costs and timeline of various informatics and technology strategic initiatives.

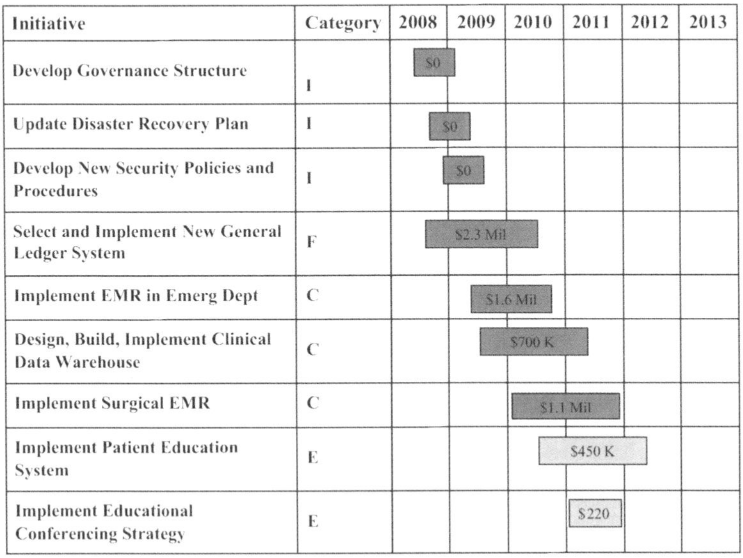

Initiative	Category	2008	2009	2010	2011	2012	2013
Develop Governance Structure	I	$0					
Update Disaster Recovery Plan	I		$0				
Develop New Security Policies and Procedures	I		$0				
Select and Implement New General Ledger System	F		$2.3 Mil				
Implement EMR in Emerg Dept	C			$1.6 Mil			
Design, Build, Implement Clinical Data Warehouse	C			$700 K			
Implement Surgical EMR	C				$1.1 Mil		
Implement Patient Education System	E				$450 K		
Implement Educational Conferencing Strategy	E				$220		

Priority	Total One-Time Capital Cost
Mandatory	$5.7 Mil
Essential	$1.4 Mil
High	$2.3 Mil
Moderate	$1.6 Mil
Low	$1.1 Mil

Categories include I-Infrastructure, F-Financial, C-Clinical, and E-Educational. Bars in dark grey are mandatory in nature. Light grey bars are essential. In the second table, the total capital costs are delineated by initiative priority.

Many examples are available of acceptable governance models. One such model is noted in Figure 8-4. In this model, informatics and technology requests involving clinical care delivery are evaluated in the Clinical I&T Subcommittee, while those requests involving non-clinical applications (i.e. financials, employee scheduling) are evaluated in the Non-Clinical I&T Subcommittee. The Technology Standards Subcommittee is responsible for evaluating all requests to assess compatibility with organizational technical infrastructure and capacity.

Figure 8-4. Representative governance structure for organizational informatics and technology.

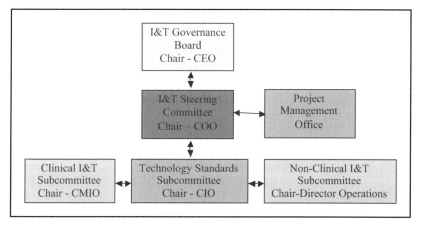

ESTIMATING CHANGES IN APPLICATION PORTFOLIO AND STAFFING

After assessing the current organizational application portfolio, industry standards, and competition and analyzing current and future gaps, an application strategy will need to be proposed which will meet current and future informatics and technology needs and be supportable. This strategy should include staffing gaps, as well as budgetary limitations. New staff planning will need to take place to ensure the success of the current and future informatics and technology initiatives.

SUMMARY

Once completed, the informatics and technology strategic planning effort should yield a robust working document, which is well-aligned with overall organizational strategy. This plan will also set the stage for subsequent planning in future years. It is important to remember that the informatics and technology strategic plan is likely to become outdated soon after it is created. The plan should be treated as a living document to be revisited and updated on a regular basis to keep up with the dynamic nature of the organization, informatics, and technology. Once established, the informatics and technology strategic plan should be widely disseminated to ensure that all staff are informed and engaged in organizational direction and imperatives.

CHAPTER 9

Meaningful Use and the CMIO, or How I Learned to Relax and Enjoy Federal Incentives

By William F. Bria, MD, FCCP

Once the final tally is over, there will probably be more new CMIO positions and people hired into them as a result of the HITECH Act than in any other event in the history of American medical informatics. You may be one of those lucky recipients of a new-found interest in a physician leader in healthcare IT by CEOs, CIOs, CMOs, and many others. This chapter will address the mixed blessing that has been bestowed on you and how to survive and succeed.

FIRST OF ALL, DON'T DO IT FOR THE MONEY!

The significant financial rewards for meeting both the hospital and provider requirements for MU have stimulated interest in American medicine in large, medium, and small settings. However, there is a growing consensus that unless you already have a mature EHR in place, it is unlikely that you will be able to meet all of the MU criteria in the published timeline and maximize your incentive dollars. In fact, there is significant risk that if you use the dollars as the raison d'être for your AMI program, you will leave important groups in the dust, dangerously compromising your overall success.

UNDERSTAND THE MAGNITUDE AND NATURE OF THE IMPLEMENTATION OF HEALTH IT

Many years ago, a nurse informaticist, Margo Cook, RN, educated me with one sentence, "Bill, don't think about the implementation of an electronic medical record system as 'technology adoption.' Rather, understand that what you need to do is most like the design, planning, and creation of a new hospital." For a young informaticist, I was a bit crestfallen, believing that all I really needed to do was to bring the "good news" of the technology era to my colleagues, and all would follow smoothly. What Cook knew is that the transformation of a medical staff and community with IT requires all the planning, communication skills, negotiation, and patience that it takes to go from planning that new medical tower to moving in on the first day. The identification of major stakeholders, the crafting of physical workspace (or virtual workspace), so that necessary natural lines of communication between providers and patients are facilitated rather than obstructed, all this and much more that I've experienced over the last 25 years in health IT has proven Cook's words very true indeed.

So for you, the new CMIO, I would ask that you consider the creation of a new medical building in your hospital. Consider the time, detail, and communication that you would need to facilitate to ensure that errors in access or safety of care are not compromised by a wall in the wrong location, for example. Further, you would want to bring together the true clinical leaders in all fields to ensure that you had the best advice on how workflow and quality of care would be supported by the structure of the new ER, that all patients in ICU could be easily seen from the central nursing station. Since what is really at stake in your healthcare setting is nothing less than the safety and quality of the care delivered to your community, I'm sure you'll quickly realize the perspective that cutting corners is hardly worth forty-four thousand dollars. Yet success could be priceless.

THE VENDOR IS A PARTNER, BUT YOU ARE THE CONTENT EXPERT

Except for the few healthcare systems in America that have developed their own EHRs, you will most likely be implementing a commercial system, setting up an important dynamic that will have significant impact on your MU program's success. One of the best aspects of the HITECH legislation is that, since it is a national program, all vendors are very well aware of the fine details of the needed functionality to meet MU at each phase of the program. Having said that, some will be developing significant new functionality for their system as a result of MU requirements. Over the years, we've been witness to more than a few colleagues who have been frustrated with their vendor relationship for a host of reasons. However, one of the most common maladies has been the "fit" of an EHR or components of an EHR with the needs of a particular health system/medical community.

Several strategies that have worked in this situation: (1) Band together! Join the vendor user group, join forces/voices with colleagues from other institutions and make your voice louder and more compelling to the vendor; (2) Befriend the CMIO-equivalent within the vendor organization—hopefully, this is a fellow physician and simply because of that fact, much of the translation that would need to occur from a vendor technologies/layman is swept aside; (3) Network, network, network! Detailed connection of you and your hospital/practices IT staff with their counterparts at other systems with your vendor product can pay dividends in problem solving, providing alternative paths to success that can come from no other source; (4) If there is no regional vendor group, make your own! Contacting colleagues in regional hospitals with the same product often forges lines of communication and relationships that result in rapid problem solving like no other strategy can. Additionally, if you have a staff, it allows you a convenient regional forum to encourage your team to present their good works and build their confidence and creativity!

YOUR DATA REPORTING ENVIRONMENT (OR IN GOD WE TRUST—ALL OTHERS PAY CASH!)

Although the implementation of EHRs in America has hardly been in existence long enough to have "traditions," there certainly are patterns of introduction of systems that are common. To introduce results reporting first, departmental systems next, and CPOE last is a fairly common pattern in the country. The implementation of a clinical data warehouse has typically been held off till the completion of this cascade, which, depending on the size and complexity of an organization, may take from two to more than five years. However, in light of the explicit and detailed data quality and safety reporting requirements of MU, the need for a robust and flexible clinical data reporting environment is now clear. Here again, the prepared CMIO can avoid a planning pitfall if he or she clearly and crisply represents the need for a robust data-reporting environment to IT. As the rollout of MU continues in America, it will hopefully be more and more common that vendors realize that to help their clients succeed, they will need to forward the need to acquire and configure clinical data repositories and reporting environments early in the process of health IT implementation.

MORE THAN A SLOGAN, IT'S ALL ABOUT PATIENT CARE

Finally, as the new CMIO approaches the task of educating his or her organization on the challenge, benefits and scope of MU, it is always important to repeat the factual mantra that this only makes sense with the goals of improved safety and quality of patient care in mind. In as much as we are in a global societal information revolution, in which data are exchanged across the globe in the wink of an eye, it is time for the CMIO to make all involved aware that the tools of true evidence-based medical practice and real-time continuous quality improvement assessment are at hand.

CHAPTER 10

Education and the CMIO

By Marc Chasin, MD, MMM, CPE

I don't know how many physicians decide during their medical training that they want to become involved in clinical informatics or set out specifically to become CMIOs. Most physicians I have interviewed migrated to this field with a keen desire to improve clinical care through the sharing of best practice and a standardization where appropriate. As a physician who has taken such a path, I have some insight as to what additional training is necessary to be credible and proficient in this new but significant role. As the field of informatics continues to develop, the number of formal informatics educational programs will continue to expand as well. Options include, but are not limited to, venues such as certificate programs, college majors, master's level degree, as well as CME and postgraduate certificate courses. This chapter will define what the properly prepared CMIO will need in postgraduate training.

Clinical informatics is an emerging discipline that melds the data analysis tools of computing with medical information and the provision of healthcare services. As more and more EHRs are implemented, the educational requirements necessary for a successful career in informatics will likely continue to evolve. Presently, there is no specific educational path to attain these goals. As we begin to define the necessary tools to become an effective CMIO, there are several essential Core Competencies you should prepare to have in your repertoire. These are as follows:

- Informatics
- Six Sigma
- Project Management
- Clinical Credibility
- Organizational Politics
- Meeting Management

INFORMATICS

The goal of a CMIO is to synthesize clinical practice and data analysis. If done well, the melding of these two sciences should improve the quality and efficiency of healthcare. Clinical Informatics is much more than the using of a personal computer or PC, but rather is seen as the ability to provide pertinent data, whether in the form of literature or other information, to the provider at the point of care. This information will benefit the individual clinician so he or she can make educated decisions based on available evidence, therefore improving the quality and safety of the care rendered.

CLINICAL CREDIBILITY

A Physician Informaticist is much more than a tech-savvy physician who likes gadgets. Although this can be an integral part of the job description, a CMIO must also incorporate his or her clinical background to maintain clinical credibility. There is much debate as to whether maintaining an active practice is necessary in order to accomplish this credibility. I will not expound on this debate here except to say that some form of clinical credibility is a must. It is important for a CMIO to understand the daily workflow necessary to render efficient high-quality care, either in the inpatient or outpatient arenas. This will facilitate an understanding of potential barriers to providing such care.

The ultimate goal is to improve throughput in any acute care setting by reducing redundancies and decreasing practice variation.

By understanding how the organization works from the inside, best practices will be easier to understand and variation can be decreased. Your credibility as a CMIO will be greatly enhanced if you can identify and improve frustrating obstacles that are encountered daily. Physicians are more likely to respond to a workflow change or introduction of new technology from a fellow physician. Since changes will likely continue at a rapid pace, the chance of buy-in is significantly improved if the proposed change comes from a colleague.

SIX SIGMA

The process of six sigma has been around in the manufacturing industries for many years. Six sigma is essentially a set of procedures and tools designed to analyze and measure "defects" in a process and help identify what's causing them. The goal, or achieving "six sigma" is 3.4 defects per million or 99.997 percent perfection. An understanding of these processes is important when working toward the goal of ultimately improving patient care.

In the field of manufacturing, if a company can produce an automobile with such perfection that only 3.4 lemons are produced per million cars manufactured, six sigma may be achieved. Six sigma comes into play in many different situations in medicine as well. There are many different treatment plans for any given illness, and the less variability there is, the less possibility of error and a greater potential for improved patient care.

In a hospital setting, it is important to understand the exact point at which errors in hospital care occur in order to appreciate the utility of six sigma. For example, it has been shown that many errors occur in transfer of care of the patient from one healthcare provider to another. A specific example of transfer of care is medication reconciliation. When medications are reconciled, a review is necessary at each point-of-care. During this time of information transfer, human error accounts for numerous errors. In this example, the role of the CMIO is to automate medication reconciliation, which will decrease errors in this transfer of care. Utilization of EMRs would therefore reduce possible defects in the process, in other words achieve six sigma.

Six sigma training involves a series of courses leading to different levels of certification. Certification is not essential but certainly knowledge of the processes of six sigma is important for a CMIO in order to reduce variability to improve patient care. Six sigma courses are available commercially, and certification typically takes six to nine months.

PROJECT MANAGEMENT

Project management is another competency with which the aspiring CMIO should be familiar. Project management is a process used to define expected timelines and project scope. It is used to focus time and resources to meet a customer's expectation on a project. Familiarity with this process will help the CMIO reduce duplication of effort, identify problem areas and risk, and serve as an excellent communication tool.

ORGANIZATIONAL POLITICS

As with any large company, hospitals have informal as well as formal organizations. The formal organization is typically in the form of a structured hierarchy that contains built-in protocols for solving routine issues. On the other hand, the informal structure is not always so easy to decipher. These are the more subliminal dynamics that involve interpersonal relationships and bonds between colleagues. When physicians are involved, this becomes more complex than a routine business top-down hierarchy. One of the more challenging tasks of the CMIO is to not only recognize that these structures exist but to then use that knowledge to get the job done. For example, it is important to know who the "nodes" of the informal organization are to expedite transfer of information or whatever the goal may be, avoiding a more circuitous and time-consuming path. Understanding these politics is particularly important as the CMIO must be able to relate impartially to all parties involved to achieve the adoption of best practices.

MEETING MANAGEMENT

Proper meeting facilitation is a learned skill necessary for anyone in business. Although meeting facilitation may not be intuitive as a physician, as a CMIO it is necessary to conduct meetings efficiently and gracefully. Physicians are typically protective of their time, and ineffective meetings can lead to decreases in attendance and participation. This could lead to loss of engagement of physicians in project development. Physicians are an integral part of the building and implementation of EHRs, and maintaining engagement is critical to adopting evidence-based practice. To preserve a collaborative atmosphere, all parties must have a chance to be heard. There must be an agenda that is strictly followed. The goals of the meeting must be clearly outlined, and tangential issues must be set aside for later discussion.

GETTING THERE

Surprisingly, even though the medical informatics field is in its infancy, there are some excellent resources to further your knowledge on many of the topics previously discussed. The American College of Physician Executives is the main professional society for physicians in management. They offer coursework through their online learning site from topics on Financial Management, Business Plans and Healthcare Informatics. Additionally they offer a professional track to their Masters of Medical Management (MMM) program. Presently this is offered through Carnegie Mellon, Temple, and University of Southern California. This degree will prepare the CMIO to make educated business decisions while maintaining the clinical credibility necessary to move an organization forward.

The Healthcare Information and Management Systems Society (HIMSS) in Chicago, IL, is also an excellent resource. Membership will provide avenues for CPHIMS (Certified Professional in Healthcare Information Management Systems) certification, as well as the ability to collaborate with like-minded professionals to discuss current issues, challenges, and possible solutions. Their offerings are extremely comprehensive and most useful in actual practice.

The American Medical Informatics Association (AMIA) in Bethesda, MD, has multiple learning opportunities including the CMIO Bootcamp. Coursework presented is challenging and truly provides an excellent outlook on the transformation of American healthcare. In addition to AMIA's 10 x 10 program, they have recently released the report "Core Content for the Specialty of Clinical Informatics," a comprehensive listing of the content necessary to perform proficiently as a Clinical Informaticist.

The Association of Medical Directors of Information Systems (AMDIS) is another important resource, and in my opinion one of the most valuable for the CMIO. This is an organization of thought leaders located throughout the U.S. that provides an outlet for the CMIO to discuss issues of concern with other physicians. Issues from single sign-on to the role of the CMIO in large organizations are candidly discussed. The professionals I have met here have been easy to approach and love to exchange best practices.

KEEPING IT GOING

There is no doubt that Clinical Informatics is still in its infancy. As the demand for superior quality of care increases and reimbursements decrease, the value of Clinical Informatics has not even seen its potential. Clinical Informatics is no longer a luxury; it is quickly becoming a cost of doing business. Succession planning is emphasized in many corporate environments, yet it is severely lacking in the medical field. I truly believe that as a society, we will continue to lag behind other nations in quality and overall cost of treatment as long as we resist adoption and proper usage of technology. Until mainstream medical education addresses and prepares future clinicians in medical informatics and clinical decision support, we will never see 100 percent adoption. True clinical quality and dramatic reduction of errors must start with education, specifically, education of physicians. As CMIOs today, I believe it is our duty to educate our colleagues on the importance of the issues discussed in this chapter to change the face of medicine tomorrow.

CHAPTER 11

CMIO—The Next Generation

By William F. Bria, MD, FCCP

Throughout this book, I hope you've perceived the excitement, dedication, and love for the challenge of becoming and succeeding as a CMIO. In this final chapter, with the hindsight of more than 35 years in this field, here are some predictions of where we are headed over the next decade or two as physicians in this brave new information world. Some of these are more audacious than others, but they are offered to not only be thought-provoking but to inspire you to develop your career in informatics to help change the role as you engage your humanist, clinical, and technical skills as you proceed on your journey.

THE CMIO WILL SUBSUME THE ROLES OF CHIEF INFORMATION AND CHIEF QUALITY OFFICER

Most every specialty in medicine over the past 30 years has been an amalgam of technology and the practice of medicine. Critical Care, Interventional Cardiology, Oncology, Radiology, etc., have all absorbed and adapted technologies in pursuit of clinical care imperatives. Indeed, the success of application of those technologies was arguably only possible with the insight and focus of clinical intelligence. From my own specialty, we have significantly altered the iatrogenic impact of positive pressure mechanical ventilation over the last 20 years as a result of going back to the principles of pulmonary physiology and mechanics: When the lung is less traumatized at a time of illness (e.g., acute respiratory distress syndrome) by high concentrations of oxygen and less airway pressure stretching those lungs, more patients survive!

So it will be with informatics, as it will become increasingly clear that IT requires deep understanding of the practice of medicine, not only for successful adoption, but more importantly, to target key aspects of health IT (e.g., clinical-decision support) in the right manner and right clinical situations to optimize the positive effects on our patients' health. Furthermore, the understanding of population, regional, and global health trends will be far more successful by individuals (CMIOs) who know not only the regulatory/compliance requirements of clinical data repository/data warehouse reporting but know also how to redesign systems to best impact medical decision making at the point-of-care. The CMIO of the future will be charged to both lead quality improvement initiatives and, more importantly, to craft the cycle of information measurement, analysis, and then design the interventions intended to improve the care process in question and re-measure outcomes.

THE BULK OF THE INFORMATION INFRASTRUCTURE RELEVANT TO THE CMIO OF THE FUTURE WILL NOT BE IN THE MACHINE ROOM, BUT IN THE HANDS OF PATIENTS

The realization in our own time that our healthcare industry is failing at treating many forms of chronic disease and that this failure is not only resulting in the highest cost of healthcare in the civilized world but also the worst outcomes has been widely acknowledged. Simultaneously, the growing revolution in portable information tools with Web access is resulting in social change (e.g., Facebook, Twitter) that is also erasing the barrier in technology between the developing and the developed countries. The Internet appears in the past decade to have mutated from a computer-centric communication medium to a person-centric one. We are already seeing a revolution from another technical field, sensors, to be revolutionizing the measurement of all manner of physiologic parameters (from blood glucose to heart rate/rhythm) with seamless connectivity to the Web and these hand-held information devices. The profundity of this change has not yet been realized but has no less potential than complete reorganization of the physician–patient relationship and the tradition of office visits, not to mention the power shift from the medical establishment to the return to the ways of era when physicians and patients actually met on a more personal and community basis.

Whatever the continuing evolution of technologies, economics, and social trends holds, it is clear that the CMIO of the future will be challenged to create a seamless information environment in which patients can both inform their physicians of their health trends and physicians can manage large populations of patients virtually. Indeed, the entire field of interoperability, with organizations fretting about the risks of information-sharing between institutions, may be soon disrupted in a fundamental way by patients having the EHRs in their hands and being the true owners of their own health data. This is certainly a long (and possibly utopian or dystopian) view depending on the reader; however, history has shown that technologies can both build empires and tear them down in the blink of an eye. The informed, agile, and patient-centered CMIO will grasp the opportunities to bend technologies to the service of patient care. To do any less results in being crushed, rather than elevated, by such change.

THE CMIO WILL BE CALLED UPON TO TRANSFORM MEDICAL EDUCATION

To date, the vast majority of efforts of incorporation of IT into the training of the next generation of physicians has been nominal at best. Sometimes it seems that the lessons of an earlier era of medicine, a time when each physician was also a scientist and trained to constantly question and test, have been lost. In the second era of The Information Age, all physicians will be challenged (some as a result of MU!) to treat their own practice of medicine as a quality improvement cycle—constantly measuring, analyzing outcomes, changing care processes, and re-measuring. The information tools to accomplish this information access and facilitated analysis are now becoming available to all physicians. It is past time that CMIOs should be leading awareness in the medical educational establishment (medical school and postgraduate) that this original responsibility of the practicing physician now needs to be reinvigorated and reinvented with tools that are as available as the smart phone. Efforts are now visible in many national professional organizations to move the dialogue on informatics from "How to optimize your office billing" to "How to better care for your patients with a data-based environment." As CMIOs, we will be called upon to lead this transition.

THE ERA OF THE "-OMICS" WILL FIRST RESULT IN CONFUSION, THEN DEMAND FOR GREATER AVAILABILITY OF CLINICAL INFORMATICS TO THE PRACTICING PHYSICIAN

Genomics, Proteomic and Metabolomics are terms that (besides just rolling of the tongue) are opaque for most physicians and their patients. That genetics appears to be resulting in just as many questions as answers in modern healthcare is born witness by the plethora of conflicting literature and medical and lay press, over the past ten years. One thing is becoming clearer however: the impact of the "-omics" on diagnosis and treatment of many (if not all) human disease is important and will ultimately result in significant modification of our previous methods of disease detection, diagnosis, and treatment. The implications of the inevitability of disease of the early era of genetics should begin to give way to the greater ultra-personalization of treatment. How much more important will data systems be when tracking populations and diseases multiplies geometrically with "-omic" subtype diagnoses? The implications for research, diagnostics, and therapeutics will obviously be profound. The skills of the physician-informatics specialist, the CMIO, will be needed as we move through this new world of knowledge as never before.

This is a wonderful time to be poised for these proposed changes and the many more that will actually occur. You have chosen a fantastically exciting time to engage in this evolution of the most ancient of arts, the art of medicine, from what may be, in retrospect, considered its stone age. With our minds and hearts firmly centered on our dedication to the quality and safety of the care of our fellow man, we are in for an amazing voyage indeed!*

---

* Now for those of you who groan at the above reference to something as geekie as Star Trek, allow me to emphasize in the words of Dr. Leonard McCoy, "Dammit Jim! I'm a doctor, not a computer programmer!"

Index